Mom,

I thought you might like to share a little in my studies. This is one of my texts for Sacramental Life.

Theo-
logy
&
Life

Studying theology is useless without putting it in practice. You and Dad have always taught me that in your own lives. Thank you for your example of MINISTRY, and showing that the Sacrament of Marriage blossoms into the Sacrament of Family. It is this example that has helped me to respond as I have to God's call in my own life.

Happy Birthday

Jim

Teaching Sacraments

by

Patricia Smith, RSM

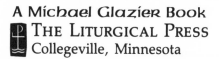

A Michael Glazier Book
THE LITURGICAL PRESS
Collegeville, Minnesota

About the Author

Patricia Smith, RSM, earned her PH.D. in Theology from the University of St. Michael's College in Toronto. She is currently Associate Professor of Systematic Theology and Assistant Academic Dean at St. Mary's Seminary in Baltimore. She has published in *Emmanuel, The Priest,* and *Today's Parish.*

A Michael Glazier Book
published by
THE LITURGICAL PRESS

Typography by S. Almeida.
Cover design by Lillian Brulc.

2   3   4   5   6   7   8   9

Library of Congress Cataloging-in-Publication Data

Smith, Patricia, RSM.
    Teaching sacraments / by Patricia Smith.
        p.   cm. — (Theology and life series ; 17)
    "A Michael Glazier book."
    Includes bibliographical references and index.
    ISBN 0-8146-5599-8
    1. Sacraments—Catholic Church. 2. Sacraments—Catholic Church-
-Study and teaching. 3. Catholic Church—Doctrines. 4. Catholic
Church—Doctrines—Study and teaching. I. Title. II. Series:
Theology and life series ; v. 17.
BX2200.S55 1990
234'.16—dc20   86-45328
                                             CIP

Contents

To my teachers at Mount Saint Agnes
and my students at St. Mary's Seminary, Baltimore—
both, teachers and learners at the same time.

Preface

Recent years have witnessed a rich outpouring of books on sacramental theology. Both in Roman Catholic and in ecumenical circles, scholars have turned from the more canonical concerns, rubrical details, and philosophical debates of manual theology to the rich and varied sources of sacramental thought and practice. Distinguished thinkers have probed the insights which the images of Scripture and the early Fathers, the relativities of history, the conserving limits of official teaching, and the challenges of contemporary philosophy offer. This book does not presume to duplicate nor even to supplement their efforts. It builds heavily on them. It is not a new book on sacramental theology as such. Rather, it is a book about sacraments *teaching* and about *teaching* the sacraments. Since 1978, I have been conducting courses on sacraments in general and on baptism and confirmation, the first two sacraments of initiation. I have offered "variations on these themes" at the undergraduate and graduate levels, to groups of clergy and women religious, and to adult groups in Roman Catholic and Protestant parishes. Many colleagues and students have found the approach helpful. A sabbatical in 1985-86 provided the opportunity to systematize and write up what I have learned from and about teaching these "focused moments" in our Christian life.

This volume presents an approach to teaching "sacraments in general." Each chapter includes samples of the kinds of questions which I ask students to think about or activities which I ask them to engage in. The central portion of each chapter consists of reflections used in class presentation. Finally, each chapter contains an annotated bibliography of readings to accompany the topic under consideration. My hope is that the content and methods expressed here will assist others in their own teaching and learning, and thus contribute to the dialogical process that is theological education. If the approach that has served me well can spark creative teaching and learning in others, then the book will have more than achieved its purpose.

In a book which is the fruit of eight years' research and teaching, acknowledgements rightfully include all my faculty colleagues and students during that time. I also wish to thank especially: Robert F. Leavitt, S.S., for his challenge to me to write during my sabbatical; Ms. Rosann Catalano, for the book's title and for shared support in the Scriptorium; Mr. Jack Lennon, for his efficient typing of the manuscript; the Sisters of Mercy with whom I lived in New Haven, for a quiet space in which to bring this writing to completion; St. Mary's Seminary students Jeffery J. Noble, Michael J. Pakenham, Blake La Mounte Sayers, and Donald M. Vowels, for proving the truth of the song, "by your pupils you'll be taught."

N.B. All Scripture quotations are from the *Revised Standard Version* of the Bible.

Patricia Smith, RSM

Fall, 1986

1

Setting the Context

I. Orienting questions and readings

Read the article on "Sacraments" in the *Old Catholic Encyclopedia,* Vol 13 (published 1913), pp. 295-305 and the articles "Sacraments, Theology of..." and "Sacraments as signs of Faith" in the *New Catholic Encyclopedia,* Vol. 12 (published 1967), pp. 806-815. Compare and contrast the ways of approaching Sacraments in these pre-and post-Vatican II formulations. Topics for comparison might include: the order and context of particular issues, sources, use of Scripture, view of the human person, historical consciousness, view of the church, liturgy, method of argumentation, definitions(s) of sacrament, weight of authority, emotional tone and language, and contemporary issues raised. In each article, what is most extensively treated? What is not there or not extensively treated? What is the instructive value of each article?

* * * * *

This exercise of comparison and contrast has been very useful. For persons without a strong pre-Vatican II sacramental knowledge, reading the *Old Catholic Encyclopedia* article provides an example of the principal categories and deductive methodology of classical sacramental theology in the Roman Catholic tradition. Those steeped in that approach see not only the clear emphases with which they are familiar. They also see the cautious openness toward ambiguity, a glimpse of recognition of historical relativity, a hint of the anthropological perspective, and magisterial understatement which are evident, even in this scholastic formulation. Knowledge of this earlier approach is of special pastoral importance for persons preparing for ministry in the Roman Catholic Church. Many of the "people in the pews" grew up with and cherished this view of sacraments. Anyone wishing to serve the faith-life of these people today must know the tradition out of which they come and reverence its power, if he or she is to communicate effectively a contemporary vision of these actions "ever ancient, ever new."

Written soon after Vatican II, the *New Catholic Encyclopedia* articles provide examples of the fundamental shift in sacramental thinking that characterizes more recent years. Once the historical-critical method is applied to Scripture and doctrinal formulations, once sacraments are taken seriously as acts of common worship, and once the theological categories of God as mystery and church as sacrament are viewed as foundational, then the stage is set for revolutionary attitudes and practice. Like the Vatican II documents themselves, these articles are transitional. They incorporate a compromise of various theological perspectives. They offer an initial, tentative move toward more inductive theological thinking and a more inclusive approach than their predecessory article. They provide "seed themes" which major sacramental theologians, pastoral ministers, and searching Christians continue to grapple with today.

II. Reflections

There is no conviction in the old priests' songs; there is only showmanship. No one in the kingdom is convinced that the gods have life in them. The weak observe the rituals—take their hats off, put them on again, raise their arms, lower their arms, moan, intone, press their palms together—but no one harbors unreasonable expectations.

John Gardner, Grendel, Ballantine Books, p. 111.

Jesus did not give his life in a liturgical solemnity — on the contrary, in an obviously secular conflict, colored though it was by religion, he remained faithful to God and to men and gave his life for his own in a secular combination of circumstances. Calvary was not a Church liturgy, but an hour of human life, which Jesus experienced as worship.

Edward Schillebeeckx, *God the Future of Man,* Sheed and Ward, p. 99.

A. SYMBOLIC CRISES: CULTURE AND LITURGY

Two directions mark a healthy sacramental attitude. One, represented by the passage from *Grendel*, takes extraordinary claims seriously. It affirms the "unreasonable expectations" rooted in belief that a saving God really is alive and well, working in and through our history. It asks of all religious thought and action, "What do we hope for?" The second direction springs from Schillebeeckx' caution not to place undue weight on what goes on in liturgy and church, unless what goes on is linked to a larger reality, a broader life context. It requires us to take ordinary things, people, and life seriously and to ask of them, "What do we allow for?" When they are really efficacious signs, sacraments (and, derivatively, sacramental theology) balance these two poles. Sacraments do offer infinite possibilities in and through the finite, the real. While rooted in the earth, they promise the transcendent. And while the bread and oil, the ministers and words that constitute sacramental acts are eminently human, their power and their promise is, in truth, divine.

It is important to set the proper context for a study of the sacraments. Even in seminaries and institutions which prepare sacramental ministers, the primary purpose of such study is not to produce proficient technicians and professional personnel. Nor is it primarily to communicate technical distinctions and definitions, important as these might be. Such study is not even to enhance one's personal religious understanding, though this may be a worthy by-product. The purpose is much broader, the need much deeper than these pragmatic, individualistic goals. In our time, the study of sacraments is particularly important because of the cultural, political, and religious crises affecting our planet. "Crisis" means not only a time of shakeup. It means a mandate for decision, akin to the meanings of *crisis* and *judgment* in the *Gospel according to John*. Industrialized civilizations of both east and west are undergoing "the collapse of traditional premises regarding the radical significance of things, the absence of any robust common faith, the turning of basic cultural presuppositions into yawning question marks."[1] Using W.B. Yeats' image of "the broken center," David Power describes our situation as a crisis of spirituality, that is, a crisis in our view of the world and of God's relation to it. In our attempt to recover both a vision of and a hope for that world, we might ask: What does modern civilization offer to humankind? What does the Christian tradition offer?

Much of modern civilization still functions out of an eighteenth century Enlightenment model. The Enlightenment offered the image of a machine — the mechanical machine of efficient wheels and precisely moving cogs, the social machine of rationalized logical thought and bureaucratic organization. Anyone who has been crushed by the technical, economic wheels of progress and/or depersonalized by bureaucracies, governmental or ecclesial, knows the inadequacies of this model. Today, men and women search

---

[1]Nathan A. Scott, "The broken center: a definition of the crisis of values in modern literature," in Rollo May (ed). *Symbolism in Religion and Literature* (New York: Braziller, 1960), pp. 178-202. Cited in David Power, *Unsearchable Riches: The Symbolic Nature of Liturgy* (New York: Pueblo, 1984), pp. 8-9.

for a more adequate human image. Scholars like Philip Keane and Kathleen Fischer plead for a recovery of the imagination, that factor which cannot be neatly confined to manageable categories. Gibson Winter uses the artistic metaphor of "human dwelling" to describe the creative energies which really enrich human lives.[2]

Many candidates vie for priority in the search for meaning among men and women today. A sacramental vision of reality deserves more than superficial attention. By a "sacramental vision," I mean a vision rooted in the earth and therefore showing reverence for the body, the environment, and God's universal, indiscriminate love for all people. In a world which *is* the Frankenstein myth, threatened by its own products and powers, such a vision is needed to counteract the human degradation, the attitude that life is expendable, the dangers of nuclear, economic, and personal exploitation. Of necessity, a vision rooted in the earth is also rooted in community and tradition. It counteracts the narcissism, rootlessness, and loss of connections seen not only in selfish solitariness ("This is my body. I can do with it what I will.") but also the despair seen in the ultimate isolation, suicide. The threads of societal relationships seem worn and fragile today. By definition, sacraments are communal actions. More precisely, they are interactions. Perhaps, in recovering their meaning, we may recover a center that is whole and that holds, a cohesive power that can sustain human beings in the fragmented and fragmenting moments of their lives.

Finally, a sacramental vision of reality is rooted in and always moving toward religious mystery. Ours is a problem-solving age. But when you have solved the last problem, what have you? By definition, the Christian sacramental tradition claims that there is more to life than meets the eye. There is always more to human beings and their condition

[2]See Philip Keane, S.S., *Christian Ethics and Imagination* (New York: Paulist, 1984), Kathleen Fischer, *The Inner Rainbow* (New York: Paulist, 1983), and Gibson Winter, *Liberating Creation* (New York: Crossroad, 1981) as examples of recent reflection on the power and necessity of the imagination in human and religious life.

than what can be neatly captured and categorized. In sacraments, things of the earth and of human creation are the primary mediators of that mystery. Mystery offers no clearcut solutions to the riddle of human existence. Rather, it affirms the ambiguity at the heart of that existence. Don Saliers describes the ". . . crucible of ordered ambiguity in our experience. The ambiguity is not confusion or disorder; rather, it is richness or experienced meaning which holds opposites in tension; dying to self and yet alive to God, renunciation yet fullness of being, remaining in this world yet citizen of another, and so on."[3] Those who embrace the ambiguity, the dimension of mystery inherent in human life are never satisfied by too-neat solutions. Their questions are never quieted by too-facile answers. Indeed, the renewed interest in symbol, myth, and the imaginative life testifies eloquently that technology is insufficient food alone for the human spirit, that precise formulations alone do not satisfy the human heart. Only conversion of the way we see, listen, and imagine determines what we shall see and hear, and whether we shall act responsibly in face of the "always more" that marks every human sign as it marks every human hope.

B. HISTORICAL OVERVIEW OF SACRAMENTAL LIFE TO VATICAN II

In the teaching of sacraments, an historical overview is always helpful. While a more detailed study may follow later, some initial and broad reflections which trace the development of sacramental thought and practice help to situate the present. Not only does an historical perspective enable individuals and communities to know where they have come from. It also provides a context for understanding why certain attitudes and practices arose at a particular place and time, and for questioning whether such attitudes

---

[3]Don E. Saliers, "Symbol in Liturgy: Tracing the Hidden Languages." *Worship* 58 (Jan. 1984): 39.

and practices remain appropriate today. Historical consciousness teaches that things have not always been the way we have known them in recent memory. This knowledge contributes to the search for what endures, sacramentally, through space and time, and to the healthy relativizing at the heart of a faith and a sacramental life which, like the church itself, are *semper reformanda.*

A survey course or text on sacraments could never do justice to the myriad details of their historical development. But the average searching Christian and the average pastoral minister need not become experts in nor get bogged down in such details, important as they may be to scholars. For purposes of manageability, Raymond Vaillancourt's broad categories provide a useful framework for an overview. He divides the history of Christian sacramental life into three periods: from sacramentality to sacramental rite (the New Testament to 1000 A.D.); the sacramental rite (1000-1960 A.D.); from sacramental rites to the sacramental nature of the church (1960 A.D. to the present and beyond).[4] This threefold division offers teachers and students of sacraments a convenient basis from which to trace the major emphases and shifts in sacramental thought and practice.

1. From sacramentality to sacramental rite (the New Testament to 1000 A.D.)

> The first Christians had no idea of "going to church" to receive the sacraments. They had every idea of "being" church, and celebrating those mysteries and festivities that brought them into contact with the risen One in their midst. They had no idea of being total sinners lining up for an injection of grace. They had every idea of being already graced through creation and through the risen One, and they gathered to express this fact in ritual and sign. They were interested in the whole community celebrating the wonderful

[4]Raymond Vaillancourt, *Toward a Renewal of Sacramental Theology* (Collegeville: The Liturgical Press, 1979), pp. 11-27.

works of God in Jesus, not in individuals privately manipulating objects to tease out grace.[5]

From their own Jewish context, Jesus and his followers inherited a complex of what might truly be called sacramental actions: blessings, ritual imposition of hands, anointing, washings, greetings, ritual meals, sacrificial offerings. These words and gestures were broad, contextualized events which *in some way* showed forth God's saving presence, God's power and love for them. These sacred signs and rituals conveyed *in some way* the very mystery of God. The qualifying phrase *in some way* is important. For among our early ancestors, there was little if any speculation on exactly how this God was present, or precisely how the divine presence worked among and for people. *That* God acted effectively through ritual words and gestures was presupposed. *How* God acted was not a burning question. In the Hebrew Scriptures, the variety of media through which God acted is staggering: through thunderclaps and a still, small voice; through faithful prophets like Isaiah and pagan rulers like Cyrus; through mighty warriors like Saul and aging women like Sarah. The Old Testament bears eloquent witness to the belief that, when it comes to God's coming among people, no one way captures that coming. No single image, figure, or gesture confines the divine presence. When the people of Israel began to "locate" God's presence too exclusively in the political structure of a monarchy and the religious institution of a temple, God taught them a bitter lesson. Exiled from these tangible securities, by the waters of Babylon they sat and wept. Undoubtedly, some despaired and abandoned their faith in the God who had promised to be with them, no matter what. But others continued to hope, to have their faith purified, and to search for new signs of the presence of their God. The post-exilic prophets bear eloquent testimony to a broadened sense of God's presence — beyond one small

[5]William Bausch, *A New Look at the Sacraments* (Mystic, CT: Twenty-Third Publications, 1983), p. 1.

tribe and in the whole of creation; beyond temple worship and in service of the poor; beyond external rituals and in the new covenant of a faithful human heart. *In some way*, these realities were genuine sacraments.

The roots of our Christian sacraments lie deep in the Jewish matrix described above. Jesus did not invent new ritual gestures. He did not introduce totally new signs of the presence and power of God. Rather, he took the familiar religious words and actions of his time — proclamation of God's Word, meals of memorial and reconciliation, a water-bath at the start of his life's commitment. He both continued the meaning that these moments had had in Israelite history and transformed that meaning in reference to himself and to the reign of God. "You have heard it said ... but I say to you." "*This* is my body." "Do this in memory of *me*." These well-known Gospel phrases give evidence that Jesus saw himself and his call as well-rooted in the richness of his religious tradition. Yet, he reinterpreted that tradition in the service of a broader mission, to proclaim God's enduring presence for and among all peoples.

Jesus certainly did not confine his understanding of the signs of God's presence to ritual gestures and specifically "religious" activities. On the contrary, if we take the Gospel texts seriously, he spent a great deal more time among the people proclaiming God's presence in word and deed than he did in synagogue or temple worship. The roots of Christian sacraments emerge from a broader context than that of formal worship alone. They also emerge out of the healing gestures of Jesus Christ himself, who used material things like touch, spittle, loaves and fish to signal the presence of God. In and through the things of the earth, God acted and human beings gave thanks. In and through the man Jesus of Nazareth, God's extraordinary power broke through in human lives. Indeed, in early Christian consciousness, Jesus Christ himself is seen as the great sign (sacrament) of God. "Who is this man, that even the wind and the sea obey him?" (Mark 4:41) "Philip, the one who has seen me has seen the Father." (John 14:9) All that Jesus said and did was sacrament, because all revealed the compassionate, faithful presence of God. All his words and deeds were holy signs, because all served to free people from their bonds of sin, prejudice and oppression.

The New Testament does not designate specific moments or ritual gestures by the term *sacrament*. In these documents, the Latin *sacramentum* is a translation of the Greek term, *mysterion*. Used especially in the letters to the Colossians and Ephesians, *mysterion* has a very broad meaning. It refers to God's plan and activity for our salvation, as revealed in Jesus Christ. It is a wide-ranging word, embracing all the ways in which God has reached out and does reach out to us in the world in and through Jesus Christ. Thus by extension, any object, action, or person that *in some way* brought God and people into contact, revealing God's saving love, was *mysterion*. Open-ended, flexible, and imprecise, the term designated any manifestation of the fulness of life and love willed by God for humankind.

Clearly, the early Christians experienced God's saving plan as revealed especially in and through Jesus Christ. More explicitly, that plan received its power through the cross and resurrection, that power mediated to believers through the ritual acts of baptism and Eucharist. By the fourth century, *mysteria (sacramenta)* came to refer to the acts of Christ himself, working through the church to manifest God's plan to unite all of creation in God's love. By extension, *mysteria (sacramenta)* came to designate the symbols and practices in which believers participated in order to enter into and be united in the life of Christ. In time and as Christianity became more established in the Roman Empire, *sacramentum* became a primary designation for the cultic celebration of the mystery of Christ, the Eucharist.[6]

---

[6]When the church began to use the term *sacramentum* more extensively, it built upon some of the word's overtones. In secular usage, *sacramentum* referred to the Roman soldier's loyalty to the national cult upon his entrance into military service. Thus, it carried the notion of pledge and promise of allegiance. Applied especially to the Christian sacraments of initiation, the term continued this notion of pledge, namely the pledge to be faithful to the demands of Christian life. This "mark of ownership" was also a "mark of commitment."

While it uses the term *mysterion (sacramentum)* in the sense described above, the New Testament is rather reserved when speaking about what are later called (seven) sacraments. The roots of these grace-filled actions are there, but not in precise form and individual, exact rituals. Jesus left no blueprints for what later becomes a sacramental system. He prescribed no personal handing down, "as is." If we take the New Testament insight into the imminence of God's reign seriously, we will not be surprised that Jesus set up no enduring institutional structures. If the end was so near, why insist on an elaborate ritual system? This is not to deny the fact of sacraments in the New Testament. There are two major foci: the water-bath of baptism and the bread-breaking of the Lord's Supper. In their New Testament context, both are moments of initiating and forgiveness. Both have to do with life in the Christian community, the Lord's Supper having especially to do with sustaining that life. But the most accurate summary of the New Testament meaning of *sacrament* is to say that this reality is broader than any specific liturgical acts. In its whole life, the community is *mysterion, sacramentum.* In its whole life, the church embodies God's plan of salvation as that plan operates in human, communal, historically recognizable form. In virtue of its being a community visible and acting in space and time, the Christian community itself has a sacramental structure. It lives out of a sacramental principle, namely the conviction that in and through what it does in history, God truly is at work in the world.

For at least the first three-hundred years of its life, the church lived with an "unthematized" awareness, a broad understanding that its entire life and behavior were sacramental. Persons, things, gestures, actions of justice and mercy were signs, sacraments of the holy. Many created realities were manifestations of the presence of God. During this early period, there was no precise concept or definition of sacramental phenomena as such. Rather, the first Christians sought to understand more fully the events of their ordinary lives by relating them more explicitly to the death-resurrection of their Lord. In time, they did focus on certain

communal human situations as especially privileged occa-
sions for proclaiming and revealing the meaning of that mystery. Entrance into their community and communal meals of
sharing and forgiveness had a priority in their lives. It is
important to note here the relationship between liturgical
celebration and the rest of existence, in the early church.
Because they viewed their entire life as sacramental, their
liturgical life was intense. As we shall elaborate in later chapters, liturgy was a "focused moment," a highlighting of what
was going on in the ordinary life of the people — dying to
sin, giving thanks, reconciling enemies, feeding the hungry.
As such a "focused moment," liturgy was a principal teacher,
a formative moment in the faith. Because the bishop was the
prime liturgist, he was the prime teacher, and not *vice versa*.
The catechetical homilies of so many great Fathers of the
Church indicate that teaching was not done separately from
liturgy. It was not simply an intellectual preparation for the
church's sacramental action. Rather, teaching was a function
of the liturgical celebration itself. Words, ritual gestures, and
symbols transmitted the faith. "Tradition" was handed on
largely in and through the assembly gathered for worship.

In affirming the church's whole life as sacramental, we also
affirm the church itself as principal agent in its sacramental
action, in those words and deeds that reveal the saving presence of God. Neither the individual nor isolated moments,
formulas, or gestures had a sacramental priority. The community as a whole tried to live as clear and faithful signs of
God's healing, universal love. What it did in its ordinary life
came to formal, communal expression in its rites. God's
self-revelation, took place in diverse ways — in prayer and
martyrdom, in receiving society's outcasts, in caring for widows and orphans. The liturgy proclaimed that self-revelation, acknowledged God's presence already at work in and
through the lives of those committed to being signs of that
presence on earth.

If we are to recover the connection between liturgy and life
and to overcome the false dichotomy between world and
worship, it is important to try to recover the attitude of our

ancestors in the faith toward their rituals. First, they viewed
their ritual moments as actions, not as things. In baptism,
what was important was not water alone. Rather, it was the
action of being immersed in water as a sign of drowning to
sin and emerging to a whole new way of life in Jesus Christ.
In the Eucharist, bread alone was not the focus. Rather, the
community's action of breaking and sharing bread was a
sign of God's sustaining feeding, in and through the breaking
open of one anothers' lives. The recovery of this verbal element in the sacraments would go a long way toward encou-
raging active liturgical participation. Seeing the sacraments
as actions, or rather as interactions, would downplay the still
prominent view that they are isolable objects, formulas and
gestures "happening" only in church and unrelated to the
day-to-day drama of human life.

The second insight from the early church worth noting has
to do with an attitude of flexibility toward ritual gestures
and formulas. Anyone who studies early liturgical texts faces
an astonishing variety of options with regard to sacramental
worship. Specific rites were not seen as *the only way* to carry
out Christian celebrations. Even what we have come to call
"the words of institution" are absent from some early eucharistic settings. Liturgical texts were viewed as helps or models, not as binding blueprints. Our post-medieval preoccupation with valid formulas and essential gestures did not seem
to be an issue for the first several hundred years of Christian
history.

In the fifth century A.D., Augustine provided the first
"technical" descriptive definition of a sacrament. Even his
definition remained broad. Augustine continued to refer to
any holy person, symbol, action, or thing as a sacrament. He
defined sacrament in two ways: "a sign of a sacred reality"
and "a visible word." In these formulations, two emphases
are especially significant. First, Augustine did not draw a
dichotomy between the sign and the sacred reality that it
signified. Sign and reality were distinct, but they were also
inseparable. This attitude is in marked contrast to a nominalist strain in later medieval thought which drew a sharp

contrast, indeed a full dichotomy, between the sacramental or symbolic sign and that of which it was an expression. This unfortunate development stands at the heart of sacramental misunderstanding articulated in the oft-heard phrase, "It's *only* a symbol." For Augustine, symbolic signs could never be reduced to the superficial connection expressed by the adverb *only.* There was a necessary, strong, and real relationship between sign and sacred reality. In its extended discussion of the meaning of *symbol,* Chapter II will explicitate this relationship in more detail. Suffice it to note here the importance of recovering Augustine's emphasis, if sacraments are to be seen as more than casual, arbitrary actions, easily dispensed with or relegated to being "extra-added attractions" of Christian religious life.

The second Augustinian insight comes from reflection on his definition of sacrament as "a visible word." Augustine viewed sacraments as a communication, a revelation from God. Thus, they partake of all the characteristics of human words (giving a message, dialogical, interactive, demanding an attentive hearer, etc.). In our time, Karl Rahner recovers this Augustinian emphasis when he describes sacraments as ". . . the highest stages in the word of grace in the Church in its character as exhibitive and as event."[7] And theologians engaged in ecumenical dialogue explore the implications of Augustine's definition as they work to break down the inaccurate and unnecessary contrast between a Protestant church of the Word and a Catholic church of Sacraments.

Our earliest history saw life, including sacramental life as one, with many legitimate expressions and manifestations. When and why did shifts in this understanding and practice occur? We can trace the significant shifts to the fourth century era of Constantine and following. At that time, Christianity not only became legitimated and accepted; it also

[7]Karl Rahner, "What is a Sacrament?" *Theological Investigations XIV* (New York: Seabury Press, 1976), p. 144. This 1971 article and Rahner's 1960 reflections on "Word and Eucharist" in *Theological Investigations IV* provide excellent examples of this theologian's grappling with the relationship between *word* and *action* in regard to sacraments.

became the established religion of the Empire. Large numbers, eventually including whole Germanic tribes in northern Europe, began to pour into the church. What did they bring? In contrast to the relatively clear personal commitment required of anyone who adopts a minority's faith-stance, they brought a blurred picture of religious motivation marked by strong political and economic reasons. In many areas, Christian feasts and sacraments took over the previous functions of pagan festivals among the people. Sacraments became not so much the ritual expression, actualization, and interpretation of Christian life, as it was when Christianity was a deeply rooted minority choice. Rather, they became means of grace for semi-pagan church members whose religious conversion was often associated with economic and political advancement. In this situation, it is a short step from viewing sacraments as means or instruments to viewing them primarily as things. And things are easily manipulable. Things can easily slip from religion into magic. Things can lose the inter-relational dimension of actions and can be viewed as isolable, personal possessions.

In the religious sphere, the rise of a clergy caste paralleled the forms of the empire's political hierarchy. This rise contributed greatly to the clericalization of sacramental practice. Ordained clergy became the experts, possessors of sacramental powers and, consequently, of sacraments. From time to time, this professional elite "dispensed" their possessions, putting the sacraments at the disposal of the masses too. But in the process, the rich symbolism of communal interaction became reduced to an over-preoccupation with rubrical etiquette, the occupational hazard of those considered both possessors of and totally responsible for the church's sacramental life. The loss of a sense of communal power and responsibility contributed to an increasing individualization regarding the "use" and usefulness of the sacraments. This in turn fostered an over-interiorization and over-spiritualization. The primary purpose of the sacraments was not the symbolic expression of a dimension of the community's life, but the eternal salvation of an individual's soul. Salvation depended more on how you acted in worship than in the rest of your life. The link between liturgy and life was diminished, if not totally eclipsed.

2. The sacramental rite (1000 to 1960 A.D.)

The historical period sketched above saw the Christian faith firmly established within society, with an enormous concomitant expansion. Evangelization of pagan tribes flourished. This dynamic continued into the second period when, in many lands, church and state were effectively one. The zeal of missionaries took both European culture and the Christian gospel all over the globe. A new dynamic emerged from "the schools" during the medieval period. This dynamic was an analysis of and clarification regarding the sacraments. The pastoral needs, especially of missionaries, to explain the faith and combat heresies in foreign lands led theologians in the great universities to ask questions that would get at the core and substance, the essential nature of sacraments. The rediscovery of Aristotelian philosophy provided intelligible categories from which to approach questions of substance and accident, source and purpose.

Two directions dominated the period of the sacramental rite from its medieval origins to its recent waning with the Second Vatican Council. The first direction resulted from efforts to formulate technical, precise concepts in response to the questions, "What is a sacrament?" and "How does it work?" Such questions seek a clear, univocal response. They contributed greatly to the standardizing of ritual. Rites which in earlier centuries (and in diverse cultural and political situations) had been relatively flexible and varied became codified into precise verbal formulas and rubrical gestures. The result was a progressive narrowing of the meaning of *sacrament*, especially in the West. Maintaining its patristic heritage of rich theologies based on imagery (by definition, multivalent) and its regional autonomy, Eastern Christianity kept the broader and varied meanings of sacramental actions alive. However, under the strong legal heritage and centralizing tendencies of Rome, Western Christianity sought one meaning for ritual gestures, one precise formula to accompany their performance. Thus, baptism became associated primarily if not exclusively with cleansing from sin. The additional anthropological and Biblical meanings of new birth, refreshment, death and life became lost. The Eucharist was defined primarily if not exclusively as a sacrifice (and a narrowly understood sacrifice, at that). The rich heritage of a communal meal, an eschatological banquet fell into the shadows. The first list of seven sacraments dates back to the twelfth century. This is less a formal definition than a statement of what, in fact, had become common practice. But its production accompanied the theological interest in questions of the institution of the sacraments, validity, causality, their correctness and efficacy, the minimal conditions regarding matter and form, and ministerial power. Philosophical developments had been proceeding out of a "contrast" mentality associated with nominalism, such that the sacramental sign and the reality of which it was an expression (God's welcoming into the new life of Christ, God's reconciling love, God's sustaining nourishment, etc.) became more and more sharply dichotomized. "It's *only* a symbol" became a sadly fitting way to describe the anemic signs of wafers in place of real bread, a dribble of water in place of dramatic immersion, a solitary gazing at the host in place of a communal meal.

The second major outcome of these medieval and post-medieval tendencies was the priority given to personal, individual action, including the personal role of the minister, be he bishop or priest. Cut off from serious reflection on their liturgical context, sacraments came to be seen more and more as instruments, tools for the salvation, in the next world, of individual souls. Questions of efficacy centered not on the moral fruits of sacramental worship, but on the correct performance of the rite itself. Though not intentionally fostered, the impression grew that there was little room for God's initiative, and that individuals earned their salvation by having certain things done correctly (formulas, gestures,

etc.) by correct persons (clergy). Popular attitudes saw sacramental grace more as a possession which one deserved
than a gift for which one should be grateful.

The merits or values of this period are evident. It gave to
sacraments the beginnings of systematic reflection, the clarity of distinctions, nuanced debate, and sharp analysis. The
period also offered the legal security of unambiguous direc-
tives, helpful especially to the sometimes unlettered missionaries who carried the Christian faith into far-flung lands.
This was a period whose richness was in its clear communication of "the bottom line."

The problems and critique of this period are equally evident. Its net result was a great amount of reductionism and
minimalism. The laudable effort to articulate the essential
core or substance of sacraments tended to reify these events
and to forget their character as relational interactions,
occurring always in a context more extensive than formulas
and rubrics, more rich than individual piety and abstract
definition. Looking at sacraments as things and instruments
eclipsed their more fundamental identity as signs of a mystery of God, a reality never able to be fully explained nor
completely contained. Their performance became associated
with trying to produce results and make things work, rather
than with serving the common, human good. Anyone who
has seen a Fellini movie with its frantic processions where
people batter one another to "see the saint" or be physically
closer to the Host knows the aberrations to which this tendency corresponds. One also sees the ritual isolation of
liturgy from the life, both of individuals and of community.
Visual imagery replaces involved participation. Sacraments
become spectacles, the faithful become spectators. And, like
pharmacists, clergy dispense the sources of grace on the
order of vitamins or, some would say, tranquilizers. These
sacred specialists hold juridical or legal power over the sacraments, a power that takes clear precedence over the rights
and power of the community of faith. The rich symbolism of
the liturgy becomes "purified" of its association with ordinary life when the simple Eucharistic table becomes an

ornate altar, the official minister is barred from marriage, ^nd the oil of strengthening for this life becomes a "pre-anointing" for the next. The question, "When precisely does it (that is, the sacrament) happen?" fosters non-attention to issues of sacramental purpose and context.

In his book on the sacraments, William Bausch presents a concrete analogy for understanding the reductionistic shrinking of symbolic meaning that marks this period. He uses our familiar North American feast of Thanksgiving.

> Suppose someone of prosaic mind tried to get at the meaning of our national Thanksgiving Day. He worked at it until at last he declared that the whole "essence" of this holiday could be captured in the turkey wing. That told it all. But, of course, what fantastic reductionism! What a poor substitute for the whole turkey itself, the whole range of long-term preparations, family gatherings, reunions, old friendships, familial visitations, renewed emotions, old joys and a meaningful spirit of what families and individuals had to be thankful for. It is conceivable that the reduced turkey wing *might* mean all of this, but surely it is a terribly reduced symbol of all that the ritual of Thanksgiving has come to mean for the American family. In fact, to carry the example one step further, it is conceivable that in due time the turkey wing might become the only symbol of the interlacing celebrating patterns of Thanksgiving Day. Future generations might well be perplexed as to what it was all about. Worse. A future generation might be content to go through some brief motion with the turkey wing in order to get on with the "real" business of life.

Something like this actually happened to the sacraments (as we shall see). In the process of analyzing them, the mystery was stripped to what some thought were the bare essentials. Then these essentials were put in the concrete of laws and rubrics. Now there was a quick and easy measurement of their validity. It was made easier for everyone to say, "*This* is a sacrament. *That* is not." It was easier to figure out precisely

> where grace resided and what to do to get it. Every person
> with rubrical savvy could call it forth. The step to magic was
> a short one.[8]

Inattention to context and to relationship between liturgy
and life, a univocal approach to multivalent symbols, a narrowing of religious responsibility to the actions of active
ministers on behalf of passive recipients: all these contributed to the loss of richness that marked late medieval piety
and post-Aquinas scholastic theology.

Today, we are familiar with the reaction of sixteenth century Reformers to the reductionist tendencies of late medieval practice and late Scholastic theology. Theirs was indeed
a rejection of the aberrations of their time. Their primary
response was a return to the biblical sources of Christian
faith. Out of this renewed emphasis, both Luther and Calvin
and their followers reasserted the priority of God's initiative
over human effort in the matter of salvation. This was a
healthy countertrend to the situation described above. Their
followers, however, continued along the Nominalist track.
They retained the contrast or dichotomous mentality that
had begun to prevail earlier. "It's only a symbol" led many to
a weakened appreciation for the biblical notion of anamnesis
and for the power of liturgy to express and evoke both the
human need for God and the divine response to that need.

3. From sacramental rites to the sacramental nature of the church (1960 to the present and beyond)

The previous historical sketch describes the long situation
that prevailed in Roman Catholic sacramental life from the
middle ages to recent times. For our purposes, "recent times"
begins with the Second Vatican Council. Many people experienced Vatican II and its aftermath as an explosion, a revolution in sacramental thought and practice which the church,
by and large, was unprepared for. While many clergy and
faithful may have been caught off guard by the council's

[8]Bausch, pp. 6-7.

direction, it is not quite accurate to say that there was no preparation for it. Several currents of scholarly thought and many pastoral questions had begun to affect the scholastic, classical view. Prior to Vatican II, three major developments laid the groundwork for the direction that this historic event would eventually take. They are: a return to the biblical, historical, and liturgical sources of our faith; the dialogue between classical and modern philosophy; and last but by no means least, concrete pastoral need.

a. Return to the sources

The nineteenth century was a fertile period for historical research regarding theological issues. This was especially true in Tübingen, Germany through the work of scholars like Johann Adam Möhler and in England through thinkers like John Henry Newman. Their studies recovered the "forgotten truth" of *development* as it applied not only to doctrinal formulas, but also the church, ministry, and sacraments. Insights from this rich period paved the way for the Mystical Body theology expressed in Pius XII's 1943 encyclical, and for the People of God image that dominates the 1964 *Constitution on the Church*. Insights and images from the first four centuries served to broaden the notion of the church beyond the largely juridical model of Robert Bellarmine. They broadened an approach to understanding the sacraments that went beyond questions of matter and form, causality, and canonical requirements in ministers and "recipients."

Biblical renewal accompanied and was informed by historical research. For years, Protestant scholars had been developing and employing the historical-critical method in regard to Scripture texts. Pius XII's encyclical *Divino Afflante Spiritu* gave the approval and impetus for Roman Catholic scholars to use this method and to study biblical passages in their original languages and contexts. One of the most important insights recovered in this process was the fact that the Scriptures are primarily the church's books of worship, and not a series of prooftexts for later theological disputes.

This acknowledgement of the close relationship between Bible and liturgy has had important results not only within Roman Catholicism, but also in ecumenical relations between Protestant and Catholic Christians. To say that the Bible developed largely out of the church's need for texts to serve its worship is to say that Word and sacrament are, indeed, inseparably united at the foundations of our faith.

A pastoral and practical observation lies at the heart of why liturgical renewal has been and continues to be so important. Most Christians never darken a rectory door for private counseling. Many never actively participate, beyond financial help, in the organized functions of parish life. Liturgy is the place in which most church members meet and experience church, most of the time. Therefore, liturgical scholarship is of utmost importance for the day-to-day life of the Christian community. In our century, Benedictines in Germany and Dominicans in France greatly widened the liturgical stream that flowed into Vatican II. Dom Odo Casel's studies of the church fathers and of early mystery cults brought forth a view of sacraments as mysteries, that is, as rites in which the saving activity of the risen Christ becomes present to those who participate in them. Dominicans like Yves Congar returned to early liturgical texts and discovered a variety of rites and images which contributed to a broadened awarenes of the meaning and potential of sacraments. "There is more here than we thought." The major official thrust to liturgical renewal appeared again in an encyclical of Pius XII, *Mediator Dei*. The new direction reached eloquent expression in one of Vatican II's most influential documents, the *Constitution on the Liturgy*, issued in 1963.

b. Classical and modern philosophies in dialogue

Since the early twentieth century and especially from the 1940s on, Roman Catholic philosophers and theologians have brought the questions and approaches of many different philosophical systems to bear on classical Thomism. Especially in Germany and Holland, scholars have used the emphases and methods of phenomenology, existentialism, and transcendental philosophy to examine the old tradition with new eyes. Each of these philosophies has a specific set of presuppositions, concerns, and a specific methodology. It is beyond the scope of this general overview to examine each in detail. However, they do have a common starting point, an interest in the human subject. Each in some way investigates the human situation, the human "conditions for the possibility" of theological doctrines, ecclesial structures, and religious practices. Two major theologians have employed these philosophical systems to great profit. Working out of a largely phenomenological framework, Edward Schillebeeckx explored the concept of sacraments as encounters with Christ, as Christ is a sacrament of encounter with God.[9] He analyzed the phenomenon of falling in love. When people fall in love, that experience reveals a reality ordinarily hidden from view. It "dis-covers" something of the mystery of another person. The common question that comes to mind when people see an "unlikely" couple illustrates this phenomenon of encounter. "What *do* they see in one another?" Whatever it is, it is only seen if and when one person enters into and participates in the life of another. Then, something new happens. The encounter effects an inward change, calling for outward response. Of necessity, it is a relational act. As applied to sacraments, the phenomenon of encounter means that these outward signs reveal a transcendent, divine reality to those who open themselves up, in faith, to a genuine meeting with God. If sacraments are to be more than external rituals, they demand a participatory engagement.

Using the resources of transcendental Thomism and Heideggerian existentialism as a point of departure, Karl Rahner developed the notion of sacraments as symbolic actions of the church.[10] He analyzed human existence and observed that human beings live in and through symbolic

[9]Edward Schillebeeckx, *Christ, the Sacrament of the Encounter with God* (New York: Sheed and Ward, 1963).

[10]Karl Rahner, *The Church and the Sacraments* (New York: Herder and Herder, 1968).

activity.[11] In every word and action, persons both say and create who they are. They both state where they are and go beyond where they were before. They embody what they are becoming. A common example: the alcoholic does not "fall into" alcoholism overnight. He or she both says "I am an alcoholic" and becomes more so by repeated and progressively addictive acts of drinking.

In its communal life, the church becomes what it is through what it does. Among its many other actions, the sacraments are what it does as part of its process of self-actualization. The seven individual sacraments are derivative of the whole church itself, which is the great sign of Jesus Christ. He in turn is the great sacrament or sign of God. Rahner's rooting of each particular sacrament in the life of the church gives a communal foundation to the sacraments that precedes and underlies the importance of individuals, including individual ministers. There is no such thing as "Father's Mass." Rather, this communal base situates individual sacraments in their larger context as collective expressions of and makers of the church's self-identity.

This ecclesial approach to sacraments has enormous pastoral potential. Seeing sacraments as actions of the church can lift the burden of an overindividualized piety. Sometimes, particular sacramental experiences do not "fit" one's religious frame of mind. There is great comfort in the realization that, like life, sacraments are bigger than we are. As actions of the church, they call us to stretch beyond our particular preferences, our familiar walls. They ask us to participate in a tradition that both expresses and transcends any one feeling or group or historical era. In this sense and at their best, sacraments are truly "catholic actions."

c. Pastoral need

Renewal, sacramental or otherwise, does not take place simply because theologians and church officials discover or

---

[11]Chapter Two explores the meaning of symbols and symbolic activity in more detail. Here, suffice it to say that symbolic activity refers to the signs (things and actions) in and through which individuals and groups both express and form their identity.

rediscover knowledge. It arises fundamentally from pastoral pressure, from an experience and articulation of need. Pastoral workers, theologians, and bishops, especially in the Third World countries from the 1950s on, asked the hard questions: Do the classical European experience, structures, and formulations fit our situation? Are they capable of responding to our concrete concerns? Admission of such questions and their implicit negative response contributed greatly to Vatican II's renewal of the church's sacramental life. Vernacular liturgies, the RCIA, flexibility in rites, adaptability to culture: all proceeded not only because old texts were newly unearthed, but also because new questions were being asked of old structures. How should the process of initiation look in areas where Christianity is clearly a "minority" choice? What historical accretions have crept in and blurred the basic meaning of the Eucharist as a covenant meal? What distorted understandings accompany the numerous addresses to Satan in the rite of infant baptism?

In large measure, Vatican II's liturgical renewal was a paring down, a search for simplicity, a getting back to and highlighting of essential sacramental signs. Clearing out the liturgical calendar, construction of altars that look like tables, giving prominence to baptismal space, a prolonged and communal preparation for entrance into the Christian community: all these and other liturgical changes happened because of real pastoral needs. Historical research and philosophical inquiry contributed much to answering those needs. But neither research nor speculation invented them.

C. LITURGICAL AND SACRAMENTAL PRINCIPLES OF VATICAN II

What happened in the renewed sacramental rites of Vatican II? What theological principles inform these events of Christian prayer? The council does not offer much in the way of a formalized, systematic treatment of sacraments as such. However, its documents on revelation, the church in the modern world, and ecumenism do proceed from a sacramental basis. That basis is the theological conviction that God does act in and through the actions of human beings in history. And the various rites issuing from the council incarnate a sacramental theology proceeding from the kinds of biblical, historical, liturgical, and pastoral factors described above.

Two principles inform the sacramental renewal of Vatican II. First, the meaning of a sacrament is found in the human situation which it expresses and to which it corresponds. Thus for example, in order to understand baptism, Eucharist, anointing, and orders, one must explore the human phenomena of initiation, eating, sickness, and leadership. What happens when any new person joins a group? When people share a meal? When you are seriously sick? When a person becomes a public leader? Vatican II takes the human situation seriously, as a theological source. It is part of the essential "matter" of a sacrament, as important as the water, bread, oil, or ritual gesture of laying hands.

A class or group exploration of the human situation is a very enlightening exercise, because many people will bring many different perspectives to this phenomenological analysis. Women, for example, will bring out the importance of preparation and followup (cleanup) in the sharing of a meal. Heads of households will describe the fear factor associated with loss of employment when one is ill. Young adults who have been members of sororities or fraternities readily recall the many different aspects of initiation. A "group, situational profile" formed out of the contributions of many persons provides an excellent starting point for the theological meaning of a particular sacrament.

The second principle informing the renewal of Vatican II is equally important, especially as it respects the relationship between systematic and liturgical theology. The meaning of a sacrament is found in the liturgical rite itself. For too long, sacramental theologians have operated within the closed world of abstract theory, and liturgical theologians have dwelt secure in the realm of ancient texts or external rubrics. Never the two did meet. Until recently, sacraments were often taught without ever adverting to the fact that these realities only occur in and through liturgical celebration. And liturgy courses often never explored the theological significance of prayer genres, rituals, and symbolic action. In its renewed rites, the council insists first of all that the normal setting for all sacraments is their celebration with an assembled faith-community. This includes that most traditionally privatized moment, anointing. It even includes the sacrament of reconciliation, though provision for the private, personal character of this event is maintained. But, whatever the variations respecting each sacrament's unique situation, in some way people are called or gathered together to celebrate, and then scattered back into their worlds to live out the truth of that celebration. The basic structure of all the sacraments is the same. First, the community gathers to hear God's Word. Second, community members respond to that Word by a particular action — being plunged into water, exchanging marriage vows, breaking bread, offering themselves for public service. The structure incarnates Augustine's view of sacraments as "visible words." The Word of God is an event. And sacramental actions do communicate.

Sacramental ritual must be seen within the larger context of life itself. When the two are authentically related, then what goes on in the life of individuals and of the community comes to expression in liturgy. What is celebrated in church reflects what is happening on a day-to-day basis in ordinary life. The language denoting at least one of our renewed rites is particularly instructive in this regard. What was formerly termed "extreme unction" or "last rites" has undergone a revolutionary shift in the understanding of its context and purpose. The emphasis is no longer on its being "extreme," but on its being "unction." But even that is not quite accurate. The 1982 revised ritual refers to this sacrament not simply as "anointing," but puts it in its ecclesial context. In 1983, the U.S. bishops approved *Pastoral Care of the Sick: Rites of Anointing and Viaticum* for use in their dioceses. The message is clear. Unless the Christian community concerns itself in an ongoing way with pastoral care of its sick members, then what meaning does the signing with oil have? Is it not magic, rather than a genuine focusing of what goes on through visiting the sick, supporting them and their families, advocating legislation for equitable health care?

This unity between life and liturgy has both positive and negative manifestations. Vibrant sacramental events generally mean, not necessarily that a worshipping group has a professional liturgist orchestrating them, but that the group has a vital ecclesial life. And those who decry the sterility of their parish liturgies should look not to these symptoms, but to the source of the problem, their overall parish life.

In its serious renewal of ritual, Vatican II acknowledges the liturgy itself, like the human situation, as a theological source. *Lex orandi lex credendi.* Our way of praying is (for better and/or for worse) an expression of our belief. This ancient formula stands both as a challenge to and a critique of the connection between how we live out our faith and how we celebrate it.

III. Supportive readings

In addition to the readings cited in this chapter, the following passages are helpful in setting a context for the study and teaching of sacraments.

—Diekmann, Godfrey. "Two Approaches to Understanding the Sacraments." In C. Stephen Sullivan, ed. *Readings in Sacramental Theology.* Englewood Cliffs, NJ: Prentice-Hall, Inc., 1964, pp. 1-17.

> Originally delivered at the Eighteenth North American Liturgical Week, this article is a "classic," a clear presentation of the shift in sacramental thinking that has marked recent times. Basing his interpretation on a positive view of authentic Thomistic theology, Diekmann contrasts Aquinas' thinking with the "unbalanced emphasis on causality" that has distorted and fostered a mechanistic view of sacraments.

—Martos, Joseph. *The Catholic Sacraments.* Wilmington, Del.: Michael Glazier, Inc., 1983, pp. 86-108. *Doors to the Sacred.* Garden City, NY: Doubleday and Company, 1981, pp. 1-160.

> The Chapter in *Catholic Sacraments* gives a broad sketch of sacraments from the perspective of their historical development. *Doors* presents such development in much more detail. Both readings provide "hinges" such as classical technical terms, especially useful for persons unfamiliar with the medieval to recent understanding.

—Power, David. *Unsearchable Riches: The Symbolic Nature of Liturgy.* New York: Pueblo, Inc., 1984, pp. 1-60.

> Power offers a broad and challenging context for approaching the current crisis of symbols in Western culture. His historical interlude also offers useful information as well as reflection on the "different ways in which symbols have been used, interpreted, and appropriated in the course of church history."

—Schultz, Raphael. "Sacraments." In Alfred Darlap, ed. *Sacramentum Mundi V.* Montréal: Palm Publishers, 1970, pp. 378-81.

> This encyclopedia article includes both an historical survey and magisterial pronouncements regarding sacraments. It is a good complement to the encyclopedic texts used in the initial exercise of comparison and contrast.

2

Anthropological Foundations of Sacramental Action

I. Orienting questions and readings

A. The following exercises are done in a group. Size is a less important factor than degree of openness and willingness of members to participate aloud. The structure of each exercise is identical: a period of quiet reflection in which participants jot down their individual responses, and a period when, in small groups or large, they share these responses with others and thereby become teachers in the educative process.

1. "What does the statement 'It's *only* a symbol' mean to you?"
This question or a variation on it is a good way to surface presuppositions, underlying understandings, and attitudes toward symbolic language and activity. Generally, responses reveal a spectrum ranging from a high regard for symbolic signs to a very casual, surface view of their import. The question brings to light the participants' present understandings of the meaning of *symbol*. This, joined with discussion of the weight of the adverb *only*, provides a foundation for building on and expanding current knowledge.

2. "What images do the following words bring to mind: water, bread, wine, oil, birth, touch . . .?"

"What happens to people when: they eat a meal together, they become seriously ill, they enter into marriage, they are initiated into a new group, they present themselves for public leadership ...?" Caution: Do not labor over responses. Jot down what comes spontaneously to mind. Do not use explicitly religious language. Think about these in their human, ordinary, day-to-day context.

When individuals have had time to formulate their own responses, choose one or two of the images and events to draw out and list the varying insights of the group. What this exercise does is to surprise people into their own awarenesses, unique and shared. It confronts them with the narrow limits of their own personal perspectives. The group responses can bring to expression the rich content of images and events, the variety of understandings which people bring to the experience of communal signs. The exercise is a springboard for a more theoretical discussion of the richness, power, and ambiguity of human signs and symbols.

B. Read David Power. *Unsearchable Riches*, pp. 61-212.

II. Reflections

A. THE HUMAN ROOTS OF RITUAL

Classical theology approached its questions first from their relationship to God or Jesus Christ. Thus, Christology proceeded "from above," starting with the divinity of Jesus and drawing certain logical conclusions regarding his knowledge, powers, and manner of experiencing his Father's love. Ecclesiology viewed the church as a true "City of God," with personnel and structures directly traceable back to the divine will. The familiar *Baltimore Catechism* definition of sacraments as "outward signs, instituted by Christ, to give grace" illustrates this point. Each sacrament was directly linked to the will of Jesus, sometimes by very elaborate proof-texting. And each was to *give* grace which meant, at least in popular understanding, to bring God's loving presence where it was not yet present.

Today, mainstream Roman Catholic theology begins not with the God whom we can presume to know only indirectly, but with human experience which, given all the cautions regarding our complexity, we can at least attempt to decipher. It seeks the human roots, meaning, and appropriateness of theological doctrines and religious practices. "From the perspective of *human* life, what are the foundations and reasons for ... the incarnation, church, grace, prayer ...?" To put our topic in terms of transcendental philosophy, "What are the (human) conditions for the possibility of sacraments?" Many theologians begin by exploring the fundamental characteristics of being human. Who are we? How do we know and become the persons we are? How do others know us? How and why do we communicate?

There are many ways in which to describe the human person. For our purposes, three observations seem most pertinent. We are embodied spirits. We are communal. And we are historical. Except in logical analysis, no one of these is separable from the other. The first is most basic and provides a rich point of departure for examining all three in the reflections which follow.

B. SYMBOL AND SYMBOLIC ACTIVITY

1. *Persons as embodied spirits: the nature of symbol*

The ancient Greeks described human beings in what came to be the dichotomous categories of *body and soul*. Modern thinkers prefer the more unitive phrase, *embodied spirit*. By it, they mean to say that human beings exist symbolically. That is, we make and use signs. This emphasis proceeds from the basic observation that our body is how we know, come to be, and communicate. Our senses, speech, and gestures are how we operate. We only know and come to be ourselves by *ex*-pressing, that is, by going outside ourselves.

Ex-pression is the key concept. This dynamic enables us to look at, to say and, indeed, to make who we are. Through externalizing our thoughts, feelings, prejudices, dreams, we both say and create a world of meaning. Different philosophical and psychological systems will have different theories regarding the causal relationship between our inside and outside worlds. Sometimes, discussions on this matter resemble the familiar "Which comes first, chicken or egg?" The causal debate is not at issue here. Rather, we begin with the empirical observation that human existence comes to its realization through signs received and given. That each person receives a name at birth; that rough or gentle parental touch largely determines a child's self-esteem and world-outlook; that children come to know and handle the world through the power of language — all of these homely examples illustrate this fact.

Signs received and given are powerful because the human mind is a symbolizing mind. That is, human beings are able to be consciously aware of what goes on both within and around us. We are not confined to the immediately obvious, the here and now. Rather, our range of consciousness extends far beyond our bodily portion of space and present moment of time. We have the capacity to imagine, to enter into worlds "outside" our own space and time. We can see in things, events, and persons an ability to point to meanings beyond themselves, beyond the immediate and evident.

David Tracy calls this characteristic "the analogical imagination,"[1] the capacity that people have to allow things, events, and persons to signify or mean something more than what they seem at first glance. While some realities seem to have more sign-bearing potential than others, all situations have a potential symbolic value. Their context is primarily determinative of this value.[2]

While the contextual basis is true, it is also true to speak about different kinds of signs. Some signs are rather arbitrary, primarily directional pointers to something else. *For*

---

[1] David Tracy, *The Analogical Imagination* (New York: Crossroad, 1981).

[2] David Power's *Unsearchable Riches* gives a thorough discussion of this contextual significance. See pages 61-70.

Sale in front of a house, the traffic cop on the corner, a parish bulletin: these kinds of signs are omnipresent in our world of ordinary, everyday affairs. Their main purpose is information, clarity, the elimination of ambiguity. We assume that the house is negotiable, that the policeman is not directing us into gridlock, and that the liturgy times are accurate. Much of life proceeds from the generally unconscious assumption that these directional pointers will serve us well.

But while these kinds of signs are prevalent, they are neither the only nor the most important ones by which we live. Some signs are more "natural," closer to what they signify than those described above. They do not exactly point beyond themselves to some other reality. Rather, they "show forth" or manifest what is there. "Where there's smoke, there's fire." For our purpose of sacramental analysis, the best example of these kinds of signs are bodily acts. They express personal, inner attitudes. They are not primarily concerned with dispensing information. More deeply, they show forth, manifest, or disclose our human needs, desires, hopes, fears, joy, and pain. They bring to expression the questions and values of our interior life, including its ultimate questions and values. They do not necessarily offer clarity. Indeed, they may invite ambiguity. We call these signs *symbols* or *symbolic activity.*

Before proceeding to delineate what a symbol is, it is important to state what it is not. In the sense in which modern anthropologists, philosophers, and theologians use the term, a symbol is not merely a sign pointing to something else. Nor do they use the term in a weak sense of only standing for an absent reality, in the way in which a statue or monument "stands for" an important person or event. Rather, a symbol is a sign which shows forth, discloses, or manifests what is there. It makes what is hidden or implicit, explicit. It is the appearance of what is already there, a sign which makes palpable or able to be experienced the reality which is (as yet) concealed but able to be revealed. The symbol makes the reality concretely available in space and time. In Karl Rahner's terse definition, "... we call this supreme and primal representation, in which one reality renders another present ..., a symbol: the representation which allows the other 'to be there.'"[3]

An example from ordinary life illustrates the point. Two people fall in love. Love is their interior attitude. How do they know or experience the other's love? How do they each express their own? Can the love be sustained if each only keeps it inside? No. A kiss is one of the most natural ways in which they express their love. The kiss does not point to something absent, we hope! It does not stand for or substitute for what is not there. Nor does it "invent" the love between the couple, though it can increase that love. When it is authentic, our outside matches our inside. In this example, the kiss is an outward sign which makes the inward feeling available and able to be shared.

Pastoral counselors should be able to catch the reverse truth in this meaning of symbol very well. Twenty years after their initial falling in love (generally a time of many and varied "signs"), the same couple comes to the parish office. One no longer feels love. The other protests, "Of course I love you. I married you, didn't I?" But a little judicious probing reveals the suspected fact: there are very few external signs of that love. It has become routine, taken for granted. And in time, in the absence of some externalized expression, it disappears.

In the sense in which we are using the terms *symbol* and *symbolic activity*, four characteristics must be noted. First, any symbol is a limited expression of that which it symbolizes. The sign differs in a way from the reality to which it gives expression, inasmuch as the sign does not exhaust that reality.[4] David Power expresses this truth in a clear discus-

[3]Karl Rahner, "The Theology of the Symbol." *Theological Investigations IV* (Baltimore: Helicon Press, 1966), p. 225. This entire article forms the basis for a great deal of Rahner's thought, not only with regard to sacraments but also with regard to the human person, Christology, and the Church.

[4]This point will be especially important in Chapter III's discussion of sacraments as symbols of God's presence, God's saving love.

sion of "negativity" and "nonidentity" between signs and things signified.[5] When the limitation or nonidentity factor is forgotten, the symbol becomes confused with what it symbolizes. You have a case of fetishism, of idolatry. You have no reason for eschatological hope. Regarding sacramental piety, you have a rigid belief that the only way God touches people's lives is through these channels of grace. Sacraments and sacraments alone fully express (and exhaust) the totality of God's love. You can't get to heaven without them.

A return to our example of the kiss points out the shortcomings of this "total identity" between sign and reality approach. If and when the kiss does come to express the entirety of the love between this couple, then their marriage is in deep trouble. Several years ago, Peggy Lee made a hit with a song, "Is That All There Is?" We might apply its title and theme to our point about symbols being limited expressions. If "that's all there is," then mystery and wonder and the thrill of not knowing desert us. Life becomes predictably boring, not to mention boringly predictable.

Like all human realities, symbolic signs are ambiguous. That is what makes them interesting. If symbols are limited expressions, they are nonetheless powerful and, in a carefully nuanced sense, necessary expressions. This is the second characteristic for our consideration. This insight lies at the heart of Catholic insistence that sacraments are efficacious signs, bringing about what they signify. While some persons and periods have affirmed this truth in an almost magical sense, the magic is not necessary. It is in the nature of a symbolic sign to make or "cause" more of the reality it expresses to be present, simply by its (the symbol's) expression. Thomas Aquinas' phrase *significando causant* enters here. By their very signing or bringing to external availability, sacraments cause God's grace to be available, more able to be experienced and, consequently, to "increase." When a kiss is authentic, it not only expresses the love between two people. The kiss increases it. People "make" love, not in the

[5]Power, *op. cit.*, pp. 70 ff.

sense that their symbolic expressions create it *ex nihilo*, but in the sense that these signs contribute powerfully and necessarily to love's continuance.

This insistence on the potency of symbols might be described as the "way of affirmation." The "way of negativity" noted above is a justified caution against idolatry. It represents the classical Protestant critique against too optimistic a view of the world, too easy an identification between God's grace and created signs of that grace. But the "way of affirmation" is equally justified, and is a particularly Catholic contribution to sacramental understanding. People do need external signs, connections between their interior and exterior worlds. We live neither by bread alone nor by ideas alone. Together, the two "ways" co-exist in a fruitful tension. Symbols are matters both of presence and absence, of concealing and revealing, of limits and power at the same time. When the tension is broken, we fall either into idolatry or iconoclasm. Neither serves us embodied spirits well.

Three other characteristics of symbols are closely related. Symbolic signs convey their meaning not by explicit denotation but by suggestion, by evocation. They work on imaginations and emotions as well as on intellects and will. Images like shared bread, a gesture of welcome, and hands layed on in blessing call forth feelings that lie deeper than rational analysis and that cannot be captured in language on the order of mathematical formulae. Because they have the power to touch the entire range of consciousness (rational thought, imagination, emotions, dreams . . .) and because in them the whole person comes into play, symbols never communicate or convince sheerly by clear logic and a necessary movement from premise to conclusion. Rather, they are effective by a different kind of persuasiveness, their ability to tap into and bring to expression those deeper values and desires that really inform our human choices, our conscious activity. We need not look for esoteric examples of this evocative power of symbols. Wherever there are human smiles and human tears, there are moving symbolic signs. In this world of random terrorist attacks on innocent people, we need only notice our reaction to news coverage of such tragedies to realize the persuasive power of national symbols like a flag-draped coffin, religious symbols like groups gathered in prayer vigil, and personal symbols like an embrace on a homeland tarmac.

Because authentic symbols correspond to these human values, desires, and needs, human beings do not so much make symbols as discover them. We do not *make* the fundamental meaning of a shared meal, nor of personal commitment. We learn it. Symbols disclose their meaning, and in that disclosure they are really like a good teacher. They invite learning. But such disclosive education is not indiscriminate. Like "reading readiness," there is a certain "symbolic readiness." It is a readiness that requires self-involvement and commitment. This is the kind of participatory knowledge which Edward Schillebeeckx described in his analysis of human encounter. Symbols do not yield their learning to cold, calculating outside observers. They can only teach those who risk entering into the dynamic of their engaging power.

By and large, we receive symbols from our cultural environment and we appropriate them in a more or less creative manner. This clearly happened in the case of Jesus, who took the familiar occasion of a farewell meal (perhaps a ritual Passover meal), reinterpreted it in terms of his life and mission, and handed it on to his disciples, his learners, in this new context. This is also the case with the early Christian communities, which adopted the washing rites of their Jewish and Greco-Roman milieus as their initiatory structures. Because of this twofold dynamic of reception and creative appropriation, symbols gain layers of meaning over time. The layers can both enhance and bury the original meaning. They can both add to the sign's evocative power and dim its primary purpose. The allegorical associations layered onto the actions of the Mass during the middle ages are good examples of the negative effects of this tendency. They submerged the primary symbolic meaning of this communal meal. People came to gaze, not to eat. Thus the need for periodic review of a community's symbols, for stripping off the excess layers to get at the original wood. Like the lines of a good classical sculpture, the most basic human symbols are stunningly simple. Welcoming a newcomer, eating together, saying "I'm sorry," gathering at moments of birth and dying: these signs endure throughout varied cultures because they transcend any one particular culture. They are capable of bearing meaning to many because they are not confined to one class, one race, one era, or one civilization.

While it is important not to burden symbols with too many layers of extraneous meaning, it is equally important to profit from their richness. By definition, symbols and symbolic activity are open-ended. They have multiple dimensions of meaning and are able to express these variations many times, in many different situations. Depending on their closeness to universal human traits or to vitally important contexts, they have gradations of intensity in their ability to show forth meaning. Tears at a funeral tend to "mean more" than tears at a football game. The group exercise suggested at the beginning of this chapter brings to consciousness this richness of symbolic meaning. What images or ideas come to mind when you hear the word *bread*, for example? Individual responses are varied and instructive for members of the group. They often express a "coincidence of opposite truths." Bread feeds people. It also gathers them together. Bread may be taken or given. One loaf is easily divided and shared. Bread is composed of many different substances which, under the proper conditions, become one. Our Biblical tradition offers reference both to bread which nourishes and delights and to the "bread of affliction." "Bread and water" is a symbol, not of healthy feeding, but of deprivation. One of the most evocative images of the action of *breaking bread* that I have seen appeared in *Jubilee* magazine during the 1960s. The words are Daniel Berrigan's. "When I hear bread breaking I see something else; it seems almost as though God never meant us to do anything else. So beautiful a sound. The crust breaks up like manna and falls all over everything, and then we eat. Bread gets inside humans." How provocative an image, with its reference to seeing when you hear. How appropriate a meditation on the fact that Jesus left, not an idea but a meal, as his enduring symbolic way of "getting inside humans."

The group exercise referred to above is really a phenomenological analysis. It is a very valuable starting-point for the study of individual sacraments. The meaning of baptism comes forth more clearly when you have explored the dynamic of initiation. Reverence both for the pain of the ill and for their mission to the well enriches the celebration of anointing for those who have imaginatively tried to put themselves in a sick person's bed.

People need symbols and symbolic activity because we need multiple ways of experiencing the world. We need the practical, functional wisdom of mathematical and physical formulae. We need the theoretical wisdom of ideas and principles. And we need the poetic wisdom of evocative, soul-touching signs.

Our analysis thus far presents a twofold role or function for symbols in human life. This double function echoes the theme of a "coincidence of opposites." First, symbols are integrative. They give expression to and offer a recognition of identity, of who and where we are. Because they can express this identity, they are capable of communicating and mediating the consciousness of human beings to one another. They can "tell it like it is." The danger in stopping at this disclosure of what is, is the danger of legitimation and accommodation. Symbols, especially powerful ones, can simply baptize the *status quo*. Thus, there is a validity both to a prophetic and a Marxist critique. Remembering the second function maintains the tension of an ongoing critique. Symbols are also transformative. They shape our identity, they make us who we are. Especially powerful symbols can radically change the lives, not only of individuals, but of whole cultures. Anyone who has seen films of the rituals of the Third Reich know this truth. Under the right (or, in this case, wrong) circumstances, words and gestures can sweep whole nations away, totally changing their direction.

For Christians, the symbol of the cross marks or identifies us as disciples of Jesus Christ. At certain times and places, its negative potential has come to the fore. It has lulled believers into a passive acceptance of the way things are, fostering a piety marked more by acquiescence than by energy. "Carry the cross — of poverty, discrimination, whatever. Your reward will be great in heaven." At other times, the same Christian symbol has been a powerful rallying point, *making* believers courageous in the face of danger. Like Jesus Christ himself, the cross has been a "subversive, dangerous memory" which will not allow history to forget its innumerable and unnamed victims.[6]

* * * * *

From the perspective of the foregoing analysis, we may describe sacraments as symbolic expressions both of who we are and of who we are becoming. We are people coming to birth and commitment, being sick and hungry, needing forgiveness, preparing to die, offering ourselves for service. Sacraments are not only statements about our present existence. They are also symbols of what we treasure from our past: the memory of what God has done "for us and for our salvation" in Jesus Christ; rites handed down from generations of those, like us, struggling to be faithful to God's call; simple gestures of a generous hand, a shared table, and a healing touch. Just as critical though often neglected in our sacramental awareness, sacraments have a dynamic, future orientation. They are signs of what we hope for. Baptism is a plunging into the "already but not yet" of our enduring life with God. Each Eucharist leaves us hungry because it is a foretaste of the heavenly banquet. Reconciliation with God and neighbor here is a shadow of the time when we shall truly be "at home."

While modern thought owes much to Martin Heidegger for his insight into the interpenetration of past, present, and

---

[6]See Johannes B. Metz, *Faith in History and Society* (New York: Seabury, 1980) for an analysis of memory as both integrative and transformative. Much of what Metz attributes to memory is equally attributable to symbols.

future in human existence, some earlier thinkers captured this same dynamic. Like the Eucharistic prayer itself, the structure of Thomas Aquinas' hymn, "O Sacred Banquet" expresses this simultaneity. In every sacrament, we give thanks for what God has done in the past (commemorative function). We give praise for what God continues to do in our present (representative function). And we live in confident hope of what God will do in the future (prognostic function).

2. Persons as communal

The preceding analysis describes our fundamental nature as embodied spirits. Implicit in the frequent plural references throughout the text is our second characteristic. We do not exist as isolated monads, alone. Though our narcissistic society sometimes eclipses this truth, we are communal at our core. We come from two other persons. From the infant's first cry to the patient's dying gasp, the relational call cries out: know me, hear me. We have a common origin and end, living in this time between only as interdependent beings. We share and discover spheres of meaning. We agree upon the meaning of certain signs like language, common memory, and a particular history. In recent U.S. history, yellow ribbons have come to mean waiting for and welcoming hostages home. In Japan, garlands of paper cranes convey the hope for peace. The point is clear. Our social situation expresses and shapes who we are together. This holds both for secular and religious behavior. Within this situation, one important expressive and formative vehicle is ritual.

Ritual is formalized, patterned, repetitive behavior. Three o'clock feedings, olympic ceremonies, a set of car keys at age sixteen, the exchange of wedding vows: all are ritual. From a psychological perspective, this repetition of signs tells us who we are. It marks key moments in our lives, preserving their impact, maintaining their meaning, and incorporating these moments into our identity. From a sociological perspective, ritual tells us who we are as social beings. Gestures, movement, words, and material objects exist within a framework of mutual understanding. Common actions express a common identity. Common meaning offers social coherence. Thus, families who gather together for birthdays, anniversaries, and holidays express and shape their family stories. Christians who break bread regularly together become the body of Christ.

Ritual plays a key role in the cultural transmission of tradition. The complex of signs and repetitive behavior presents a context wherein groups recall the event which called them into being (July 4 as the birthday of a country, anniversaries as the birthday of a family, the Exodus as the beginnings of the Israelite people, the Last Supper as founding moment of the Christian church). Some such behavior is so powerful that, through a memory which brings past into present, the behavior "effects" presence at that archetypal event. Thus, ritual puts successive generations in touch with their founding persons and moments. It both expresses and creates the group's identity, building up an "apostolic succession" of new members.

In its formalized and repetitive behavior, a group not only expresses and maintains contact with its past history. It enacts and hands on its values. It renews and communicates its mission. It brings a future into being, reflecting not only what the group was and is, but what it hopes and strives for. Ritual has the power to pull successive generations into a group's common purpose, its challenge. Karl Marx called a certain brand of religion the "opium of the people." Another brand, expressed and fostered through ritual, is the "adrenalin of the people." Mexican farm-workers gained strength by marching together behind the banner of Our Lady of Guadalupe. Followers of the Ayatollah Khomeini fuel the fires of their zeal by repeated chants to Allah. Jews in the Warsaw ghetto found strength to resist the Nazi machine by the unending recitation of their creed, "Hear, O Israel."

Especially when performed in a professedly sacred context, the theological function of ritual is no less important than its psychological and sociological aspects. Formalized, predictable behavior offers a sign of objectivity, much needed in an age when subjective feelings have been raised to prominence. The tradition of ritual provides a structure, a "given" that shapes and guides attitudes. The role of ritual is not so much the expression of personal feelings, though this can be a useful by-product. Rather, it is a quiet, long-term disciplining of attitudes toward God, the self, and the world. Theologically, ritual offers an experience of self-transcendence, because it invites participants to enter explicitly into a larger whole than their immediate, personal world. The predictability of a certain order and a certain set of roles need not be stifling. Predictability can free persons to enter into the full dynamic of life, which is always larger than this moment, this feeling, this need. Anyone who has participated in an anointing of the sick or attended a funeral knows the freeing power of ritual. In moments when we tend not to have words or the composure to say what is in our hearts, the church offers us its words of lament and hope.

In both a humorous and an eloquent vein, a recent *Time* essay expresses this self-transcending function of ritual. "The Hazards of Homemade Vows" describes the danger when bride and groom express their commitment in language totally unrelated to the common meaning of marriage and the common universe of discourse surrounding this event.

> "Gina," the minister intoned, "do you agree to love Peter more than you love chocolate?" The bride said, "I do." After that touch, Peter's promise fell a little flat. "Peter," the minister asked, "do you agree to love Gina more than the morning newspaper?" The bridegroom looked into his bride's eyes with a smile of insufferable whimsy: "I do."

The essayist's closing remarks capture what ritual, sacred or secular, is all about.

> If bride and groom repeat the same vows their parents repeated, the vows they may expect their children to repeat,

and if the same tears are shed now that were shed five generations before at the same rite, then the ceremony has its continuity and resonances. The formality may be boring, but it is not meaningless.

If the bride and groom have intimacies to whisper, there are private places for that. A wedding is public business. That is the point of it. The couple are not merely marrying one another. They are joining the enterprise of the human race. They are, at least in part, submitting themselves to the larger logics of life, to the survival of the community, to life itself. They enter into a contract with processes deeper than they can know. At the moment of their binding, they should subsume their egos into that larger business within which their small lyricisms become tinny and exhibitionistic. The ceremony dignifies the couple precisely to the degree that they lose themselves therein. The mystery of what they do is more interesting than they can ever be.[7]

Needless to say, ritual must never be allowed simply to become rote, uninformed by personal commitment. Of its nature, ritual (including liturgy) is conservative. This is a value, especially in a fast-moving age like ours. But ritual must also be living. It can only remain so by retaining involvement in the actual life experience of those who celebrate it. A common temptation is to allow ritual to become the possession of a small portion of a community, the experts. Others become passive attendants. Thus, the necessity for theological education as well as ritual revision. Whose Mass (church, mission, etc.) is it anyway? Each age must ask the question: do these symbolic signs, these ritual moments accurately express what is happening in people's lives? Does this context really communicate what the sacrament intends to communicate? Symbols are not unambiguous. For many people today, the Eucharist is less a source and summit of

---

[7]Lance Morrow, "The Hazards of Homemade Vows." *Time* (June 27, 1983), p. 78.

unity than an occasion of alienation. The situation cannot be blamed simplistically on lack of faith or the presence of ill-will. A recent volume in the Concilium series raises serious questions. Can we always celebrate the Eucharist? Are the conditions for expressing any unity present? Is a particular celebration a source of hope for unity beyond the obvious divisions of racial and sexual discrimination?[8]

Symbols partake of the same ambiguity as human existence as a whole. Both are open to multiple interpretations. Such interpretations may be conflicting. It is the role of liturgy not to suppress or cover over the conflict, but to allow it to come to expression. Again, if symbols, including sacraments, are signs of what is, then what is conflictual must be included in their celebration.

In summary, sacraments viewed as ritual moments are communal signs of who we are together. They both say and create, express and transform our communal lives.

3. *Persons as historical beings*

The final characteristic of our human existence and symbols is implicit in the remarks above. We are historical-concrete, situated in a particular place at a particular time. Martin Heidegger describes us as "thrown" into existence in the condition of limited freedom, making our lives within the limits of finite possibilities.

Because the past, the present, and the future are simultaneous dimensions of human existence, elements both of continuity and of change exist in us simultaneously. We are at once both the same as and different from what we were yesterday. And, a very important reflection for those who live within a religious tradition: we are at once the same as and different from people of other space and time. Rahner puts it well when he says that the "man of today" is never merely the man (or woman) of today.[9] Certainly, our histor-

---

[8]Mary Collins and David Power, eds., *Can We Always Celebrate the Eucharist?* Concilium, Vol. 152 (New York: Seabury Press, 1982).

[9]Karl Rahner, "The Man of Today and Religion." *Theological Investigations VI* (Baltimore: Helicon Press, 1969), pp. 3-20.

ical situation poses unique problems and possibilities. Medicine, mobility, nuclear energy, world food production and distribution, TV satellites, political terrorism: all affect our religious, sacramental experience because they "make" a world significantly different even from our recent ancestors'. The exponential rate of change will only accelerate that difference. And yet, human beings today still have the same basic hopes, hurts, desires, relationships. They still want someone(s) to know and love them, to respect their worth. They still want a decent life for themselves and their children. Again, this one human existence lived out in myriad moments exemplifies the "coincidence of opposites" that is our life.

History and culture are major factors in theological development — the formation, deformation, and reformation of religious formulas, attitudes, practices. So much more the need to see liturgical rites as *semper reformanda*. What is of universal and lasting importance in our practice? Where are there accidental accretions? What signs cloud the deepest meaning of a particular sacrament? What signs clarify it? Is the primary sign of the Eucharist the elevation of the sacred species or a shared table? Is the essential ritual gesture for Orders the "handing on of the instruments" of chalice and paten to say Mass or the laying on of hands, signifying a share in pastoral leadership?[10]

The historical factor is important not only because of who we are but also because of who God is. Judaism and Christianity are eminently historical religions because the Judeo-Christian God acts in and through history. In recent years, much has been written contrasting the characteristics of an

[10]The choices made in recent liturgical revisions answer these questions in favor of certain ritual gestures over others. The principle upon which such changes are made is not always articulated. By exception, Pius XII in his Apostolic Constitution *Sacramentum Ordinis* (1947) expresses the principle by which he declares the matter of the sacrament of orders to be the laying on of hands alone. "If the same handing over of the instruments has at some time been necessary, even for necessity, in virtue of the will and precept of the Church, all know that the Church has the power to change and abrogate what she has determined." Cited in J. Neuner and J. Dupuis, eds., *The Christian Faith* (New York: Alba House, 1982), p. 506, number 1737.

historical religion with those of a religion based on nature's cycles. In the former type, history itself is a theophany, a disclosure of the God who moves and moves people forward. History, including change, is not a threat when God's caring presence is an abiding conviction.

Wolfhart Pannenberg's emphasis on history as anticipatory and teleological, shaping us from our end and not simply from our origins, has tremendous import for sacramental reflection. We remember our past in virtue of what we anticipate as future fulfillment. Animated by this perspective, people can be comforted rather than threatened with the provisional nature of everything now, with the truth that nothing now exhausts the final possibilities.

The "negative" dimension of our historical nature is the stark reality of our human limitation, our finitude. We humans need to struggle to integrate the many, often conflicting forces that mark our existence. Like ourselves, our signs are finite. They are never a perfect fit, either for ourselves or for God. This awareness should counsel us both to be patient and to move freely beyond a particular limitation. It should encourage humility because the transcendent can be identified with no one created reality. It should inspire confidence because, with all our finitude, God chooses us to work and to be signs of the divine presence on earth. This "both-and" dynamic of our finite thrust toward the Infinite mirrors the death-life, light-dark, bitter-sweet simultaneity that is human life.[11]

. . . .

The turn to the subject implicit in this analysis of our human situation is not new. Thomas Aquinas himself theologized that certain aspects of the sacraments were "fitting" to the nature of persons. The current concern for the human foundations of sacraments illustrates the twentieth century version of the pastoral principle deep in our tradition:

[11]In his article "The Real Absence," Donald Gray gives a clear exposition of the "already and the not yet" dimensions of sacramental reality. See *Worship* 44 (Jan. 1970), pp. 20-26.

sacramenta propter populem. Sacraments are for the sake of the people, and not vice versa. When we take our human characteristics seriously, this maxim becomes a critical standard in relation to laws, policies, proscriptions, etc. At times, we have viewed these central symbolic acts primarily as rewards for virtue, often demanding an unreasonable level of perfection. Many in our grandparents' generation took this so to heart that they would never think of going to communion on Sunday unless they had "gone to confession" the day before. But if the Eucharist is really the meal of pilgrims, then it is not reserved for those who have "arrived." If this meal is food for our common journey of faith, then who should partake more readily than those who struggle daily to live that faith in an increasingly complex world? The principle, "sacraments for people," puts the question of Eucharistic reception for sincere Catholics in second marriages in a pastoral perspective. Not "are they worthy" but "do they need sustenance?" Even the question of Eucharistic reception for baptized infants takes on new dimensions when we admit that, on a human level, parents do not wait to feed their children until the children know, in a conceptual way, the meaning of food. To vary our earlier theme, is the Eucharist a reward for correct knowledge or a formative factor in growth into full Christian life?

Critical questions about sacraments have emerged today, not simply within a personal faith perspective. They come at us sharply from within the framework of social justice, of institutional oppression. Liberation theologians challenge a heavily sacramental religion. Sacraments: of *what* are they efficacious signs? What positive power have they shown in making individuals and societies more human? Bernard Cooke rightly asserts, "To broaden one's capacity to live with various symbolisms is to deepen one's capacity to exist humanly."[12] But do these symbol systems change things for the better? Do they energize people to struggle against discrimination, to tackle harmful structures? To return to an

[12]Bernard Cooke, *Sacraments and Sacramentality* (Mystic, CT: Twenty-Third Publications, 1983), p. 51.

earlier point, are they opium or adrenalin? Monika Hellwig's short volume on the Eucharist puts the critique in sharp focus. "...the real problem is to find whether the Christian gospel has anything to say in response to the social questions of our day (that is, the questions that arise out of urgent and widespread human suffering today)."[13] In the individualistic preoccupations of our medieval past and self-absorbed present, we have forgotten that all Christian gifts are for others. Like Jesus Christ, sacraments are for *us* and for *our* salvation. That includes being freed on a human level from bondage to unjust economic, political, and ecclesiastical systems. That includes a social struggle against social sin.

Grappling with the human meaning of sacramental signs leads into a new approach to the canonical preoccupation with the conditions for sacramental validity. The term *valid* comes from a Latin root, meaning *powerful.* If sacraments "work" largely through their sign-value (*significando causant*) and their persuasive mirroring of life, then they are valid when the power, strength, and creativity of authentic life shows in the sign. They are valid when God's redeeming presence in *this* human moment shines through. Needless to say, this notion places in jeopardy the sacramental validity of perfunctory rituals performed by uncaring ministers amid blatantly biased congregations. It places the issue of validity in a broader-than-canonical context, with a broader-than-canonical challenge. It moves the issue away from preoccupation with who is or is not officially ordained and what formulas do or do not make the sacrament happen, and into the realm of what human difference any of this makes anyway.

[13]Monika Hellwig, *The Eucharist and the Hunger of the World* (New York: Paulist Press/Deus Book, 1976), p. 2.

III. *Supportive readings*

— Bausch, William. *A New Look at the Sacraments* (Mystic, CT: Twenty-Third Publications, 1983), pp. 13-31. This parish pastor offers a clear, simple treatment of the role of ritual in human life.

— Cooke, Bernard. *Sacraments and Sacramentality* (Mystic, CT: Twenty-Third Publications, 1983), pp. 4-55. Cooke presents a thorough discussion of symbols and their grounding in human experience. His approach offers an interesting contrast to that of David Power in *Unsearchable Riches.* Both deal with many of the same foundational issues. But Power's book is more technical and suited to more academically-oriented readers. He uses the philosophical insights of Paul Ricoeur to interpret sacramental symbols. Cooke's gift for clarity comes through best in his use of many concrete, down-to-earth examples to illustrate the sometimes abstruse points raised in philosophical and theological discussions. His book serves a general readership well.

— White, James F. *Sacraments as God's Self-Giving* (Nashville: Abingdon Press, 1983), pp. 13-33. This noted Methodist liturgist gives an excellent analysis of "The Humanity of the Sacraments" and a clear presentation of the meaning of *signification.* His reflections bringing together *words* and *actions* offer a service to ecumenical dialogue.

3

Theological Foundations of Sacramental Action

I. Orienting questions and readings

A. This is an individual and group exercise similar in structure and purpose to that suggested in Chapter Two. What is your favorite image of God? Why is this your favorite? What positive values does this image contribute to an understanding of the kind of God we believe in? What are its limitations? What is your definition and/or image of grace? What are the definition's positive values? limitations?

B. Read the creation stories in Genesis (1:1—2:4 and 2:5—3:24) with a view toward their significance for sacramental thought and practice. What do these two accounts have in common? How do they differ?

II. Reflections

Within our Judeo-Christian tradition, theology explores many specific questions. What is the Church? petitionary prayer? the meaning of suffering and death? In fact, all of its questions are variations on a single theme, the relationship between God and people. Biblical writers name that relationship *covenant*. The preceding chapter probed the meaning and necessity of sacraments in relation to one pole of that relationship, the human person. This chapter looks at the other pole, God. For believers, the most basic religious question is not "Do you believe in God?" The issue is "What *kind* of a God do you believe in?" Corollary questions follow. "How do Christians understand God and God's gift of grace? How do we view the structure of creation? What language best expresses the reality and presence of God to humankind? What impact do our fundamental affirmations about God have on our sacramental understanding? Why sacraments?"

A. JUDEO-CHRISTIAN IMAGES OF GOD

For centuries, our faith tradition has been bedevilled by an overly abstract preoccupation with an overly abstract God. Categories borrowed from ancient Greek and Roman philosophies have dominated discussion and debate. The Absolute, the Eternal Idea, Being Itself, First Cause: these and similar noun-terms have accompanied the adjectival descriptions of omniscient, omnipresent, and omnipotent. But the image of an Unmoved Mover has not proved to be too religiously moving. The biblical renewal cited in Chapter I has sent theologians back beyond the Platonic, Aristotelian, and Stoic terms to our primary source, the Scriptures. These varied texts from different periods and places have yielded much fruit both for theological reflection and for religious inspiration.

1. The experience of God

The Bible is not a neutral set of documents. Varied as its books are in style, content, and stages of theological development, they all work out of the same basic conviction: at the heart of all reality, there is a particular kind of God. Biblical writers use many different images to convey some aspect of this God: mighty warrior, mother, father, lover, shepherd, judge, friend. Each includes a dimension of the total truth — that this kind of God is powerful, caring, watchful, and demanding. Underlying all the images is a presupposition, not to be taken for granted when one compares the Judeo-Christian deity with others in the ancient world. This God is not capricious, not inimical to humankind. One has only to recall the familiar Greco-Roman myths to know the opposite. These Olympian inhabitants enjoyed tricking poor mortals. They liked to embarrass creatures, to catch them in an act of human weakness, to watch them "twist slowly, slowly in the wind."

But the God of Jews and of Jesus is not like that. While ever a demanding God of righteousness and justice, this deity is caring, forgiving and, many times, suffering with the people. This holy God calls people to be "the image of God," and therefore to be holy too. The first chapter of Genesis develops this holiness motif well. As an outflow of God's love, creation itself is not a static "thing." Rather, the world, especially the human world, is a mandate to continue that holy love. The prophets expand and specify the scope of this holy love. Caring for widows and orphans, restoring land to the poor, suffering on behalf of others: this is being holy, as God is holy. In his life and message, Jesus continues the motif. Not those who cry "Lord, Lord," but those who do good to others are the creative, holy ones. Probably no scene has captured popular imagination better in this regard than Matthew's depiction of the Last Judgment (Mt. 25:31-46). Here, God's blessing is not contingent upon the number of prayers said, but on a correct reading of signs. The hungry, thirsty, imprisoned, and alienated are signs of God. To care compassionately for them is to be holy. Those invited to enter eternal life *are* so invited because they have bettered human life.

The whole biblical story plays out the drama of God's love offered to and often rejected by humankind. God freely enters into covenant. In that binding, God gives instruction (Torah, the Law) that spells out mutual expectations. This instruction is more than a mere series of what to do and what not to do. It is a revelation, an act in which this God communicates God's very *self.* Amid all the varied emphases of the scriptural texts, the biblical God comes across as someone who keeps promises. For this reason, despite the prevalence of pain and suffering, Jewish and Christian believers hold to an essential trustworthiness at the heart of the world. God is not out to get us. Nor is life. God is "for us." So is life.

No less fundamental than the fact of a caring God, another conviction grounds our religious tradition. More basic than any and all images is the truth that God is mystery. We Christians hold that, in the flesh and blood of the man Jesus, the God of caring love has come irrevocably among people. But even in that coming, this God remains a permanent and abiding mystery.

In an earlier time, religious educators often used the category of mystery as an answer to questions. How many adults recall the stock reply, "It's a mystery!"? A mystery was primarily something you could not understand. Therefore, you should not ask any more questions about it. Today, mystery is still an appropriate framework in which to situate questions about God. But this is not because there is nothing more to learn from the question. This is not a convenient device for closing off discussion and debate. On the contrary, mystery denotes a very active, persistent questioning. It invites reflection because there is always more to probe, to learn, and to give oneself over to. Belief in a God of mystery does not stifle the human mind, but expands it.

Key biblical texts testify to this conviction that mystery lies at the heart of human and religious experience. Exodus 3:13-14 is a good example. Here, we learn the name that God revealed to Moses on Sinai. The situation is very human. Moses asks the natural question of a spokesman concerned with what information he shall convey to those awaiting him back at the camp. "Who are you? What are you called?" The answer is enigmatic. We are all familiar with the translation, "I am who am." Those conversant with the linguistic possibilities of Hebrew render the text "I am who I will be." More question than answer. Imagine the plight of Moses, tromping back down the mountain with that message. The very self-revelation of God is a revelation of enduring mystery. So much for facile slogans that proclaim, "God is the answer!"

But the Israelite experience of God does not begin and end with mystery, especially a mystery that remains remote from human history. This mysterious God enters into life. "I will be for and with you." There is a crucial insight to be gained by reading the Hebrew Scriptures carefully. God promises abiding presence. But God promises no limiting specifics on the manner of that presence, no information on exactly what that presence entails. God does not delineate *how*, only *that* the loving presence will be there for people. In the Bible, God's presence equals favorable assistance. "I am ... as mercy, forgiver, judge, deliverer, beacon of hope ... whatever you need by way of consolation and of challenge." Israel's history is the gradual unfolding of this mysterious name, the gradual dawning that their God is both known and unknown, revealing and concealing, among and beyond them — at the same time. Like themselves, their God is an ambiguous " coincidence of opposites." Their God is always more.

In the New Testament, the variations on this theme of mystery focus around the person of Jesus. The Gospel refrain, "Who is this man?" conveys the point. He is Jesus of Nazareth — neighbor, son of a carpenter, child of Mary, teacher, and friend. He is bold prophet and compassionate healer. But he is more. "Even the wind and the sea obey him" (Mark 4:41). A thorough analysis of the biblical meaning of mystery in relation to God and Jesus is beyond the scope of this work. But each page of the Scriptures gives more questions than answers, more impetus to searching than to satisfaction. Each writer gives witness to the unfathomable and, therefore, ever more fathomable mystery that is God.

What is at stake if one takes this foundational theme seriously? If God is abiding mystery, then God is never an object or a "thing" that humans can grasp. God is a paradox — both known and unknown, grounding and drawing us forward. God is *un*-definable, *in*-exhaustible — a reality so profound and so rich, that there is always more.[1] Because this transcendent mystery can be identified solely with no particular reality, the primary human awareness is one of restlessness and longing. How is the longing stilled? It is not, at least not completely. It may be assuaged at times, but never totally satisfied. That is both the bane and the blessing of the human condition.

In our century, the Benedictine Odo Casel first brought this *mystery* theme to the fore of theological consciousness. But the strain is not new. Great mystics like the Eastern Fathers, Pseudo-Dionysius, John of the Cross, and Teresa of Avila struggle to express the inexpressible mystery that grounds their religious experience. Classical theologians like Bonaventure and Aquinas stand in awe of what exceeds their clear, precise categories. The ringing critiques of John Calvin and Karl Barth stand out as eloquent testimony to the God unconfined by human concepts. David Power's "way of negativity and non-identity" is a recent articulation of this truth. On a pastoral level, realization of the Jewish and nuclear holocausts that marked World War II forced theologians out of their neat Scholastic certainties. The only adequate answer to such horror was an enduring search. Theologians recovered the theme of the *latens Deitas*, the hidden God. While eclipsed at times in theological thinking and religious practice, this forgotten truth has resurfaced today with great appropriateness. At what other time in history have so many global and personal unknowns faced us? At what other time such need for a God who is enduring question, who walks with people through the myriad questions of their lives?

2. Language about God

If *this kind* of God does reveal and communicate lovingly, and if *this* God is always more than people can know and

---

[1]This insight corresponds to the analysis of the theologians like Karl Rahner, who describes the essence of human life as self-transcendence toward the absolute mystery, God.

express, then a correlative question follows. What kind of language is most capable of saying who and what this God wants to be for us? What signs are most "fitting?"

The answer to these questions should be clear. As with human beings who are relative mystery, so with God who is absolute mystery. Symbolic signs are the best we have. Analogous, mythopoetic words, gestures, and objects are most fitting, because they too both reveal and conceal at the same time. With this kind of God, when all is said and done, all is *not* said and done. We have only allusions, hints of an explanation. Short of face-to-face immediate contact, all that God has and all that we have for expressing the inexpressible are signs: God communicating in a way that does justice to God's self-identity and in a way that humans can receive. If God is always known in relation to us, then God is known through creatures, through symbolic signs. A burning bush, a preceding cloud, a man on a cross, bread broken and wine poured out: this is the symbolic tradition of which we speak. Just as such signs are not an arbitrary matter with regard to human beings, neither are they such with regard to God. Avery Dulles puts it succinctly: "God cannot manifest himself to us except by making signs that are perceptible in the created order. We see God not as He is in Himself but as reflected in the things that are made." (Rom 1:20)[2]

Often, theological reflection on revelation and on sacramental symbols have occurred in relative isolation from one another. But a closer look discloses many common notions that bind these themes together. Both God's self-communication and symbolic signs are about revealing and concealing at the same time. Both revelation and symbols have a transforming effect on those who give themselves over to their power. Both influence commitment and behavior. Both the revelation of God and the symbols of that revelation introduce people to realms of knowledge inaccessible to discursive thought alone. Both offer a "surplus of meaning"

---

[2]Avery Dulles, "The Symbolic Structure of Revelation." *Theological Studies* 41 (1980), p. 60.

beyond the obvious. Both invite participants into their respective movements and carry the participants beyond themselves. Both are a "coincidence of opposites" in the manner in which we have used this phrase above.

We may rightly speak of a revelatory structure of sacraments, as well as a sacramental structure of revelation. In and through its worship life, a people comes to know its God and its God comes as truly present among them. By definition, neither the people's knowledge nor the symbolic presence exhausts all that there is to the mystery of God. Both the knowledge and the symbols are humble servants of and witnesses to that abiding mystery.

An additional descriptive definition of sacraments emerges from reflecting on the nature of God as mystery. Sacraments are signs of the presence of and communion with the God who, by definition, is beyond every fragmented grasp and limiting word. They never resolve the ambiguity between finite signs and infinite God. They are both sign and countersign at the same time. They never solve the mystery. Rather, sacraments are tangible signs that the mystery of God abides at the heart of human life. That mystery is loving. Commitment to this kind of God means that you can be faced with life's ultimate and enduring questions, and still say *Yes*.

Living out of this truth should free sacramental participants from any semblance of compulsion, scrupulosity, or pride. That includes official ministers. It should mark sacramental religion with reverence and a committed search to radicalize, purify, and simplify ritual expression. Rahner speaks frequently of a "sober realism" with regard to any religious claim or theological insight. This caution especially applies to sacraments. If they are signs of the abiding *mystery* of God, then they must elicit religious modesty in face of that mystery. On the other hand, if they are signs of the mystery of *God*, then the divine presence is indeed *real* in them. These symbolic expressions are effective signs, because God does what God says. "I am . . . and I will be with you."

3. Pastoral implications

The pastoral implications of belief in a God of mystery are enormous. How do our acts of worship and the actions of our lives invite commitment, not to neat certitudes, but to enduring search? How do our signs of liturgy and of life respect the mystery of God's presence? How faith-worthy are all our symbolic expressions?

Sacramental religions have often and justly been accused of lulling people into a false security, a comfort based on a narrow reading of the signs of God's presence. I recall the priest's statement after my infant cousin's baptism: "She's worth more now than when she came in here." A medieval superstition both illustrates this propensity toward magic and indicates the valued members of that society: a woman would have a boy-baby if she gazed at the Host on the day she gave birth. In earlier times, many people ran from church to church out of a drive to "get in" as many Masses as possible. Today, more and more informed believers question any traces of these kinds of attitudes and behavior. They ask: does our sacramental worship initiate into mystery, that is, help people to go beyond their well-known values, securities, fears, and achievements? Or is this worship self-serving, offering false comfort and a flight from the real, hard questions that human existence faces us with? Does our symbolic expression help expand people's sympathies and transform their lives and structures? Or is it more like an insurance policy, ever reinforcing the *status quo?*

The original sin of a sacramental religion is to try to deliver God, to package the mystery. The dangers inherent in a highly-developed system of rubrics and in people's security needs make this clear. But the critique of the 16th century Reformers is pertinent here. The function or service of sacraments is not to placate or put us at ease. It is to face us with our radical need for our "undeserved" God. Correspondingly, the function or service of sacramental ministers is neither to inject hypodermic needles of grace nor to act as religious filling stations. It is to issue an invitation to believers (including themselves) to open up to the basic mystery and question that we all are and, more basically, that God is. Far from setting us into a false security, sacramental worship should be a stimulus to transcendence, to moving beyond where we are. It is the theological foundation for the human willingness to risk. Rather than being cozy stopping-points, sacraments are way-stations on a common pilgrim journey. On that kind of journey, the clearest certitude is the misty light of faith.

The validity of Christianity as a symbol system depends on the power of a double dynamic. It depends on a sacrament's capacity to evoke and share a human experience (Chapter Two). Just as important, it depends on that same sacrament's capacity to evoke and share an experience of the mystery of God (Chapter Three). In this dynamic, the human and the divine do not grow in inverse proportion to one another. On the contrary, the more a sacrament expresses the human condition, the more it expresses the reality of God. And the better it reveals a dimension of God's presence, the better it reveals our human need for and participation in that presence.

With its global devastation, World War II brought the consciousness of God as mystery to the fore. This category remains appropriate for our generation and, if tendencies proceed as they are, for those in the foreseeable future. Family breakups after years of marriage, random atrocities in the wake of terrorism, massive unemployment, uprootings of whole groups of people: all are experiences of great uncertainty. Rather, symbolic signs should help people to live well with the daily uncertainty of their lives. They should foster commitment not in spite of, but in face of the questions. If sacraments are based on the conviction that the ultimate mystery, God, is friendly to us, then they have nothing to fear. Nor have we.

A sacramental church and its ministers do not exist to give airtight answers. They are a sign of shared hope in the benevolent mystery of God, and of commitment in the face of that mystery. The church does not say "Take religion three times a day and the pain will go away." Rather, like the

God of whom it strives to be a sign, the church says: "We are — and we will be with you, no matter what or how."

This is a humbling realization. We do not grasp God. God grasps us, and holds us fast in a presence "already given." We are gifted with the mystery of God, but we are not that mystery's sole possessors. We are servants of the mystery, not its manipulating masters. We are charged with preparing the soil and human conditions for its disclosure. We are called to expose this Good News, not to impose nor to hold smugly onto it.

B. UNDERSTANDINGS OF GRACE

1. Biblical insights from the Book of Genesis

No scholar employing the historical-critical method of research would hold that a biblical text intends to present a systematic theology. But the eye of a theologian can discern, in biblical passages, themes that contribute to fruitful theological reflection. If sacraments are created signs of God's presence, then it seems legitimate to examine the two creation stories of Genesis 1:1-2:4 and 2:5-3:24 with an eye toward their sacramental potential.

Every biblical text has a literary form and a religious content. In Genesis One, the two are mutually illuminating. "The medium is (a good part of) the message." Framed in liturgical language by the Priestly school, the form of Genesis One both emerges from a worshipping context, and serves it. Genesis One is a myth. This literary genre is most fit for attempting to express the inexpressible: the relationship between God, the absolute mystery, and God's people. Myths use stories and symbols to probe realities so deep and so pervasive that "everyday," prosaic language will not do. Genesis One is dramatic — a carefully constructed scenario of words which effect, and actions which proclaim. God spoke ... and it was done.

Like this first creation story, sacraments presuppose and

occur in a liturgical context. Like all authentic religious expression, they proceed from and are directed toward the abiding mystery at the heart of human existence. They are symbols evoking and deepening the relationship between God and people. Structured through words and actions, they continue to proclaim and to effect God's presence in the world. In the Hebrew perspective, words and deeds are often synonymous. Both are powerful and effective signs, extensions and real expression of the one speaking and acting. Both are modes of communication, and both are capable of bringing about what they proclaim. The sacraments are "efficacious signs." These word-events really do make present what they signify. "And it was so." (Gen 1:7, 11, 15, 24, 30).

The theological content of Genesis One reveals aspects of creation which have a direct bearing on sacramentality. In the Judeo-Christian tradition, the world is not a random, capricious happening. The Babylonian creation myth recites the birth of their gods. But Genesis One focuses not on the divine being, but on the *world* as a deliberate overflow of God's goodness. The whole world order is the first sign of this goodness. In the words of the poet Gerard Manley Hopkins, "The world is charged with the grandeur of God." Vatican II enunciates this theme when it calls the church "sacrament of the world." Even before a particular people is "chosen," the cosmos is consecrated, by the good and holy God.

A particular historical tradition does focus and interpret the meaning of creation. The entire book of Genesis is related to the central Hebrew religious symbol, covenant. The first creation account is read back, after and out of the Exodus experience. In Genesis One, God's initial act (the conquest of primordial chaos) becomes the first in a long series of saving actions, the initial sign of power and care. This creative ordering is presented as the model for God's (later) act, liberating and forming the community of Israel: first in their escape from Egypt, and later in their return from exile.

The sacraments make explicit use of material creation's capacity to "sign" to God. They are rooted in a broad vision: the world is good and holy, because it is created by the good God. As particular historical traditions within that world, Judaism and Christianity focus that cosmic goodness. They do not exhaust it. As particular moments within the Christian tradition, sacraments illuminate the holiness "always, already" offered in and through the world. They are not discontinuous with it. They do not magically "import" grace into a world untouched by God's power and care. They point to the meaning of the whole created order, which God saw was good.

Like our God, the sacraments are "for us, and for our salvation." This is the confession of the Christian community. Sacraments are communal actions, actions first and foremost of the entire church. Each is rooted, historically, in the religious awarenesses growing out of the Exodus. Each is meant to liberate — from selfishness toward community, from fear toward commitment, from self-satisfaction toward conversion, from chaos toward meaning.

In Genesis One, creation means more than "things called into being." It is more than a once-and-for-all event. Men and women are fashioned in the creator's image and likeness. Therefore, they are called to do what the creator does. The covenant establishes a dynamism: the commission to continue, as partners, the ordering of the universe. Human beings are to continue the creative event through their fashioning, through their signs. Thus, they continue to express and to effect God's powerful, saving presence in the world. This material world is the means whereby God's power, wisdom, and care are manifest. The earthly becomes a sign and a promise of the divine.

The sacraments continue creation's dynamic movement from and toward God. They are human signs, effected and participated in by human persons. But these persons are made in the image and likeness of God. Image and likeness is not only a gift. It is a responsibility. "And God blessed them, and God said to them, 'Be fruitful and multiply, and fill the earth and subdue it. And have dominion' . . . " (Gen 1:28). In the sacraments, men and women not only rejoice in their gifts. They pledge to use them responsibly. They promise to be transformed, and to transform their world into an authentic image and likeness of God. "Mundus semper reformandus" is no less a Christian task than "ecclesia semper reformanda."

In cosmic terms, Genesis One portrays a majestic, powerful, transcendent God. Cosmic creation is a gift from and a sign of this God. If we only had the creation account of Genesis One, we would be left with only a lofty, cosmic view of "the way it is." But human experience is not so neat. There is another side. In their wisdom, the Israelites and early Christians included in their canon a second account of their origins. Chapters Two and Three shift the emphasis. Out of the early Yahwist tradition, this narrative focuses on human creation: man and woman in their relationship, amid their problems, their day-to-day living out of the human condition. This story introduces the note of ambiguity: creation is good, but it is fallen. The man and the woman try to exceed the bounds of their humanness. Again, in Hopkins' words, the world "bears man's smudge and shares man's smell." Thorns and thistles, sweat and sorrow enter the scene. In this narrative, the everyday aspects of the human condition come to the fore. Adam must work hard to make a living. Eve must bear children in pain.

Even in this human predicament, creation and the creator God remain positive realities. Human creation is primarily a sign and the locus of Yahweh's care and involvement. "It is not good that the man should be alone: I will make him a helper fit for him" (Gen 2:18). Here, God is someone familiar. The deity stoops down, walks in the garden, makes clothes, and searches. "Where are you?" (Gen 3:9). An all-powerful deity doesn't ask that kind of question. A concerned God does. In the second creation story, God is truly "down to earth," abidingly present in the midst of ordinary, everyday life.

The sacraments express and effect God's loving concern

for those images marred yet marvelous, human creation. Sacraments embody the fundamental Christian conviction: God is both beyond and among people. These sign-events encompass the whole of human existence: its cosmic, critical moments (birth, death, commitment . . .) and its daily routine (being nourished and nourishing, loved and loving, forgiven and forgiving . . .). Bread and wine, water and words, oil and hands are "earthly" signs. It is in this earthly life that God is encountered, or not at all. In our present historical existence, human signs are the only means that God has to speak to people (and that includes the Incarnation of the Word). And human signs are the only means that people have to speak to their God. "The Lord formed man of dust from the ground" (Gen 2:7). From the ground, from the signs of this earth, men and women continue to be formed.

What do these texts teach us about sacraments, God, and grace? First, they present the two-fold revelation at the heart of our faith. God is a being of majesty and power, and cosmic creation is a sign of this. God is also very down-to-earth, caring for and interacting with people. Human creation is a sign of this. Both Genesis stories must be taken together. They present a God whose self-gift, grace, is both power and care. That grace does not enter a neutral world. God's grace works in the ambiguous arena of a world and people good and fallen, gifted and flawed at the same time.

Our sacramental system mirrors the dynamic of these cosmic and everyday poles. In general, several sacraments correspond more to the "peak" moments of life. Baptism, confirmation, marriage, anointing, orders: these focus God's grace given and received in special times, "key" saving events in the lives of individuals and communities. Other sacraments focus God's grace in a more "everyday" vein. The Eucharist and reconciliation, in particular, correspond to the daily, ordinary needs of people for nourishment and forgiveness. Most of life is lived out in non-dramatic moments, the times "between" the relatively few peak experiences. God's self-gift is no less present here.

The second insight which both Genesis stories offer is an

equally important one. Creation is not a static, one-time event. The world, including the human world, is an expression of the covenant between God and people. That covenant demands ongoing commitment, a share in God's mission of ordering and caring for the world. God's grace is not only a gift to humankind, but a responsibility. If sacraments are signs of God's grace, then they too are not only gift, but responsibility. Such an awareness keeps participants in the sacraments far from the temptation to "settle in" to a comfortable religious piety. It energizes them for the long haul of self-giving "even unto death," that is God's promise and challenge to the world.

2. Contemporary theological emphases

Biblical scholarship is not the only factor informing the church's thinking about God, grace, and their relationship to humankind. The enduring pastoral question asks, "How do we understand God at work in our world?" Given the global awareness brought on by mass communication and travel, the question includes a very specific interest in God's relationship to all persons, Christian and non-Christian. Are all graced with the presence of God? If so, how so? If so, why bother with a specific religious tradition? Why sacraments?

Vatican II did not present a systematic theology of grace. But its documents, especially the *Dogmatic Constitution on the Church, Pastoral Constitution on the Church in the Modern World, Decree on Ecumenism,* and the *Decree on the Church's Missionary Activity* proceed from a significant shift in understanding. Two major presuppositions characterize this shift. The first is that grace can still be grace even when and if God distributes that self-gift generously throughout the world. The second is that while nature and grace are logically distinct, they are, in the concrete order of life, inseparable.

Karl Rahner's theology of grace lies at the heart of the contemporary understanding. Rahner speaks of a "supernatural existential" that is a constant in all persons — a permanent, primordial orientation toward God. In the concrete order of persons, there is no "ungraced nature," no deprivation of God's grace until or unless one deliberately blocks that grace by a culpable choice. The problem in understanding and accepting such a starting-point is that we are used to thinking in oppositions, in terms of either/or. Either we are natural or supernatural, creatures either of nature or of grace. Such dichotomous thinking forms the basis for a popular view of God's grace as the "layered look," piled on top of our human nature like a coating, an extra-added attraction for those chosen by God to rise above their human condition. But while grace remains radically distinct from the necessities of our human reality because it is *God's* gift, grace is also an intimate dimension of that same human reality. Nature and grace are distinct, but inseparable. In the concrete, the natural and the supernatural orders are radically one.[3] In the poetic words of another twentieth century thinker, "by virtue of the Creation and, still more, of the Incarnation, *nothing* here below *is profane* for those who know how to see."[4]

Another Rahnerian emphasis informs much of today's theology of grace, and the relationship between grace and sacraments. This is the continuum between unthematized awareness and gradually thematized expression. In Rahner's analysis, deep within all persons lies an infinite longing for the God already there, a dim and gradually growing consciousness of one's identity as creature in relation to the ultimate mystery, God. This awareness must come and gradually does come to explicit expression — through words, rituals, commitment. What is inside us seeks externalization. This externalization is not confined to personality traits, psychological attitudes, etc. It includes God's

[3]Many of Rahner's foundational writings proceed out of this insistence on the inseparability of nature and grace. See especially "Concerning the Relationship between Nature and Grace," *Theological Investigations I* (Baltimore: Helicon Press, 1961), pp. 297-317 and "Nature and Grace," *Theological Investigations IV* (Baltimore: Helicon Press, 1966), pp. 165-188.

[4]Pierre Teilhard de Chardin, *The Divine Millieu* (New York: Harper and Row, 1960), p. 66.

grace. One of Chaucer's characters quipped, "Murder will out!" A Rahnerian would add, "So will grace!"

In all of this discussion, we must acknowledge that the term *grace* is and has been a multivalent concept within our tradition. *Grace* has signified the relationship between God and people, expressed in the biblical category of *covenant*. It has denoted both the offer of and the result of that relationship between God and people, emphasizing the character of grace as *gift*. And, while the term has at times been viewed somewhat as a thing which God gives to some people, it has meant primarily God's gift of *self*, God's *self*-communication to people. This last meaning corresponds to the Scholastic category of "uncreated grace." It is the foundational meaning for a contemporary understanding of grace. Not a thing but a person, the very self-gift of God.

Picking up on the unthematized-thematized point made above, for Rahner and other theologians sympathetic to this approach, God's self-gift of grace is first experienced not in a thematized way, not in explicitly religious moments. Rather, grace is first known in the human spirit's stirrings beyond self and toward transcendence. Those stirrings can be in very prosaic moments. Nevertheless, "When we have let ourselves go and no longer belong to ourselves, when we have denied ourselves and no longer have the disposing of ourselves, when everything (including ourselves) has moved away from us as if into an infinite distance, then we begin to live in the world of God himself, the world of the God of grace and of eternal life."[5] This awareness of the God already at work in our lives grows and comes to conscious expression in boundary, limit, or "focused" situations. These may or may not be explicitly religious. They are always eminently human.

This shift in a theology of grace attempts to overcome the extrinsicism that has marked much of the theological enterprise since the period of late Scholasticism. A dichotomous view of nature and grace has resulted in a view of grace, at worst as anti-human, and at best as super-human. Neither

[5] Karl Rahner, "Reflections on the Experience of Grace," *Theological Investigations III* (New York: Seabury Press, 1974), p. 89.

direction has served an integrated spirituality well. Four points mark this shift, linking it with other shifts in thinking about God, Jesus Christ, and the church. First, the current position insists that grace is *God's* self-communication, offered always and everywhere, in and through the depths of human existence. The radical opening up of the whole person toward his or her authentic humanity *is* the radical opening up of the whole person to God. In this sense, grace makes us more human, not more than human.

Second, grace is capable of and indeed oriented toward concrete, historical manifestations. Grace may be "structured" in and through finite expressions. For example, God can and does communicate and touch people in and through sacramental actions. However, God's self-offering is neither confined to nor exhausted by specific groups or events. This corresponds to the earlier insistence that symbols express but never exhaust a reality, and that certainly no human sign exhausts the reality that is God. There is always more of the healing, sustaining, challenging love of God than even the powerful efficacious signs that are sacraments can express.

Third, grace is pre-eminently an event, not a thing — the inexhaustible mystery of God revealing, communicating in and through our history. We Christians believe that the supreme instance of this offering is the human event of Jesus Christ, an event of compassion, healing, and courage that spanned his lifetime, culminating in the ongoing self-gift that is the cross. But even Jesus does not exhaust God's love.

> Jesus is not atypical of what God is up to in the world: God is not out of character in his self-revelation in the ministry and fate of Jesus — he is in fact most in character, most himself ... Jesus is indeed the great sacrament, the great sign, the great symbol of God's self-communication to his creatures, a self-communication which is not isolated here but which is rather focused here.[6]

[6]Donald Gray, "Sacramental Consciousness-Raising." *Worship* 46 (March 1972), p. 134.

Fourth, God's grace is always, already present before it is consciously recognized and brought to thematic expression. This means that God's self-offering is capable of being accepted. In popular language, we call this acceptance *grace.* It is also capable of being rejected. We call this rejection *sin.*

Through those who formulated its documents, Vatican II picks up an ancient theme articulated by Saint Augustine. In his thinking, God offered and communicated life, love, and grace *non ponentibus obicem,* to those not placing an obstacle to it. This view informs Augustine's defense of the practice of infant baptism since, presumably, infants could not block God's grace. Traces of this Augustinian insight occur in various conciliar documents. Two statements are especially striking. In discussing the relationship of various categories of persons to the church, *Lumen Gentium* states:

> Those also can attain to everlasting salvation who through no fault of their own do not know the gospel of Christ or His Church, yet sincerely seek God and, moved by grace, strive by their deeds to do His will as it is known to them through the dictates of conscience. Nor does divine Providence deny the help necessary for salvation to those who, without blame on their part, have not yet arrived at an explicit knowledge of God, but who strive to live a good life, thanks to His grace. Whatever goodness or truth is found among them is looked upon by the Church as a preparation for the gospel. She regards such qualities as given by Him who enlightens all men so that they may finally have life. *(Constitution on the Church,* Article 16)

In affirming the common "religious sense" found among all peoples, *Nostra Aetate* reiterates this positive theme.

> From ancient times down to the present, there has existed among diverse peoples a certain perception of that hidden power which hovers over the course of things and over the events of human life; at times, indeed, recognition can be found of a Supreme Divinity and of a Supreme Father too.

Such a perception and such a recognition instill the lives of these peoples with a profound religious sense. *(Declaration on the Relationship of the Church to Non-Christian Religions,* Article 2)

3. Pastoral implications

The implications of such a theology of grace are great. They touch all areas of Christian thought and practice. First is the humbling recognition that members of the Christian community are not the only "graced" human beings. God's life lives in all who have not willingly rejected it. Second, the Christian Gospel is not "news from nowhere." Rather, this news is good precisely because it responds to and expresses what human beings already know and experience in the depths of their heart. A third implication related to the two above is most pertinent to our considerations. Sacraments are not the only "channels of grace," not the only holy moments in human life. They are among the many instances of God's loving presence to people.

The image which such a theology suggests is that of *focus,* rather than of isolation. The church is a body of believers who, in their lives, focus what God is doing throughout the world. The Gospel brings into clear focus the questions, longings, and needs of the human heart. In ritual words and gestures, sacraments focus what God is always about in those who open their lives to the divine healing, feeding, welcome, and call to commitment.

If there is a revolution in our theology of grace, there is a corresponding revolution in our theology of sacraments. If this is true, then we must seek a new understanding of the relationship between grace and sacraments, a new purpose for sacramental activity. Put sharply, do sacraments *bring* grace and make holy what is otherwise not holy? Or do sacraments *focus,* help us to recognize and acknowledge God's grace-filled presence already operating in human life? In an article valuable as much for its clarity as for its comprehensiveness, Donald Gray answers in favor of the second option.

It is in life itself that the issue of salvation is decided and it is precisely by living life that one runs up against (this) redemptive mystery ... The sacraments, rightly understood, do not summon us out of life for an encounter with the divine mystery in a world apart, but rather send us to the experience of life itself. The sacraments light up for us what is taking place in all of life; they are a focusing of the divine creative and redemptive activity at work everywhere.[7]

In this framework, grace is the condition for the possibility of any sacramental, liturgical event. Before we celebrate, God's promise and love are already at work, enabling us to do so. This insight reinforces the point made in Chapter II about taking the human situation seriously. In the depth and mystery of ordinary life works the depth and mystery of God.

The corresponding truth is also important. Based on an analysis of our human condition, we may affirm that God's grace does seek historical expression. God's self-revealing love does tend toward a "signed presence." Sacraments are the church's expression of this presence. They are signs which enable people to bring into focus and recognize what is "always, already" going on in the world. It is instructive to reflect on the fact that a primary biblical and patristic symbol for baptism, the Eucharist, and Jesus Christ himself is light. Light does not bring something totally new to a situation. Rather, light enables a better recognition, a clearer experience of what is already there. Light allows an increased awareness, such that better recognition may transform the situation. Things are and aren't the same, after the lights go on.

Beyond insurance of salvation, a new necessity grounds the response to the question, "Why sacraments?" Human beings need light. In our lives, historical concrete expressions are not only a need. They are an inevitability. Grace (God's unthematized presence) and history (the thematized expres-

[7]*Ibid.*, p. 138.

sion of that presence) are reciprocally necessary. We need signs given and received.

We also need the awareness that sacraments are important moments of the intense focusing of God's loving presence, though not the exclusive possession of it. In the sacraments, the ongoing dialogue between God and people is "brought to light." But the dialogue goes on in times and places outside these telescoped moments.

The church and its sacraments are a community and events that live out of a certain consciousness. These people and these moments have not cornered the market on God's loving presence. Rather, they have recognized and proclaim in a "visible word" what human existence is all about — that there is a radical religious dimension to *all* of life, that human beings are always both holy and sinful, always both made in God's image and in need of reform.

The preceding remarks have attempted, briefly, to sketch out the major points of a contemporary theology of grace. Today's insights have not emerged without a great deal of theological debate and technical meaning. Our Western literary tradition includes some expressions that also affirm the priority of grace, the presence of God which grounds and makes possible recognition of that presence. Augustine's phrasing is probably the most familiar. "You have made us for yourself, O God, and our hearts are restless until they rest in you." By definition, we are restless only for what we already, even dimly, know. The seventeenth century thinker Blaise Pascal put it this way. "You would not seek me, if you had not already found me." Again, we seek what we already know. Finally, the twentieth century poet T.S. Eliot captures the point.

> We shall not seek from exploration
> And the end of all our exploring
> Will be to arrive where we started
> And know the place for the first time.
> ("Little Gidding," *Four Quartets*)

Sacraments evoke and express what is deep within us because, at their best, they are signs of "coming home."

Like the insights deriving from recognition of the power yet limits of symbolic signs, those deriving from belief in a God of mystery and a grace already active in life suggest "ministerial modesty" with regard to sacraments. The human contribution to the dialogue is not "to make God happen." Rather, it is to allow God's already active and loving presence to disclose itself, to break through. In this sense, sacramental ministry is very much like teaching. Good teaching does not so much put new information into students' heads, like a bank deposit. Rather, the good teacher prepares the soil, fosters the conditions that allow and encourage learning. Occasionally, something clicks and the light dawns.

Both teaching and sacramental ministry are humbling tasks, demanding genuine acts of faith from those who engage in them. Both demand a personal investment, a giving oneself over to the unknown. The effects of learning are not always immediately discernible. Nor are the effects of sacramental worship. Like Pascal, those who teach and those who minister "wager" that God is there, and will be there at the end.

III. Supportive readings

—Dulles, Avery, *Revelation Theology*. New York: Herder and Herder, 1969. *Models of Revelation*. Garden City, NY: Doubleday and Company, 1983.

> Dulles' 1969 work presents a valuable historical overview of Christian views of revelation. From Old Testament views to selected twentieth century authors, he spans the centuries, giving greatest weight to his treatment of nineteenth and twentieth century thinkers. *Models of Revelation* takes up where *Revelation Theology* leaves off, in that it is a systematic inquiry into the nature of revelation. The chapter on

"Symbolic Mediation" (pp. 131-154) is most pertinent to questions of sacramental theology.

—Haight, Roger. *The Experience and Language of Grace.* New York: Paulist Press, 1979.

This introductory text surveys "the historical landmarks in the theology of grace" in our Western doctrinal tradition. Chapter One, "The Experience and Language of Grace," (pp. 6-31), is especially helpful for surfacing the various meanings, popular and technical, associated with this central theological category.

—Rahner, Karl. "The Concept of Mystery in Catholic Theology." *Theological Investigations IV* (Baltimore: Helicon Press, 1966), pp. 36-73.

Rahner wrote the three lectures that comprise this article in 1959. It is one of the "foundational" expressions of his thought. It includes discussion of numerous issues pertinent to sacramental theology, most notably the mystery that is the human person, the ultimate mystery that is God, and God's self-communication "in the concreteness of the incarnation and grace."

—Two recent articles in Leo O'Donovan's collection of essays, *A World of Grace* (New York: Seabury Press, 1980) elucidate Rahner's thought.

Anne E. Carr's "Starting with the Human" (pp. 17-30) explores the mystery that is the human person. It is an excellent "translation" of Rahner's analysis of the person as transcendent spirit. Michael J. Buckley's "Within the Holy Mystery" (pp. 31-49) explores the goal of the transcendent human spirit, namely the mystery of God. Buckley succinctly expresses the positive meaning of mystery as "not that which I cannot know," but "the endlessly intelligible."

—John Galvin's "Grace for a New Generation" *Common-weal* (Jan. 25, 1985), pp. 40-42, is

> a brief but clear summary of Rahner's achievement in formu-
> lating a theology of grace which "safeguarded the free divine
> initiative and yet avoided seeing grace as a foreign element in
> the universe, extrinsic to the world in which we live" (p. 41).

4

Christological Foundations of Sacramental Action

I. Orienting questions and readings

A. The following statements frequently occur in discussions of the relation between Jesus Christ and the sacraments:

> "Jesus instituted the sacraments."
> "Jesus Christ acts in the sacraments."
> "Jesus is a sacrament of God's presence."

How do you understand each of the above?

B. Read the following New Testament passages with a view toward their possible significance for an understanding of sacraments:

> John 1:1-18; 20:1-21,25
> Mark 16:1-8; Luke 24:13-52
> I Corinthians 15:3-58

II. Reflections

A. CONTEXT

In classical sacramental theology, discussion of the relationship between Jesus Christ and the sacraments dealt primarily with one issue. While theologians did speak of sacraments as "actions of Christ," their main interest was historical. They sought to demonstrate the connection, generally direct and immediate, between the historical Jesus and the "institution" of the sacraments. They employed biblical texts to prove the link between a moment in Jesus' earthly life and the beginnings of each of the seven sacraments. Today, in the light of historical-critical research, we know that much of this prooftexting stretched the context, meaning, and intent of these texts. Given the fact that the Gospel stories circulated in particular Christian communities for years before they were written down, scholars are very careful not to claim too many "very words of Jesus." Given the fact that Synoptic accounts of ostensibly the same event differ, they are cautious about claiming exact historicity. Given the fact that Jesus' preaching of God's reign seemed to proceed out of apocalyptic expectations that "the end time is near," it is difficult to posit his intent to institute a sevenfold sacramental system.

Mainline scholars generally agree that the pre-resurrection Jesus did gather a group of followers and sent them out to do as he did — to heal and preach the reign of God. His followers continued to do so after his death, first in small local communities and, gradually, in the late Pauline terminology of the "great church." These local groups had varying practices with regard to structure, ritual, and their community life. They had no uniform timeline of development. In the sense that he gathered disciples and involved them in his mission, Jesus founded a church. In and through this church, he instituted sacraments, as the ritual expressions adopted by this visible community acting in space and time. Only the rites of baptism and the Lord's supper are possible "immediate" exceptions to this "mediate" institution. From a biblical perspective, only they have a direct correlate to a moment in the life of the historical Jesus.

An ecclesiological foundation for the institution of sacraments does not remove all Christological questions. Indeed, it shifts these questions from their earlier historical framework to a genuinely theological one. Building on the insight that grace seeks historical expression in space and time, theologians look to the claim that Jesus Christ is the fulness, the sign and focus of all the good that God is doing in the world. This contemporary theme builds on the Pauline images of Christ as the firstfruits of a harvest to follow, the firstborn of a creation which , in time, will burst forth in fulfilment. It has roots in the Johannine view of Jesus Christ as the revelation, the one through whom we see who God is.

In examining the relationship between Jesus Christ and the sacraments, sacramental theologians today follow many different approaches. Some reverse the process which has prevailed since the Council of Chalcedon. That process was a Christology of descent, a Christology "from above." The divinity of Christ having been clearly affirmed, certain logical deductions followed. This included full knowledge of all things actual and possible, in the consciousness of the historical Jesus. Many scholars today, more informed by biblical roots than their fifth century predecessors, prefer a Christology of ascent, a Christology "from below." They examine the phenomenon of Jesus as the Gospel writers, especially the Synoptics, portray him. They probe the sign of his words and deeds and proceed, largely inductively, to a deeper awareness of what he signified. This approach takes the myriad questions that surround Jesus in the Gospels seriously. The questions point the inquirer beyond the obvious identity of this carpenter's son, to the enduring mystery of his life and person. "Who is this man, that even the wind and the sea obey him?" (Mark 4:41) This Christological inquiry is a variation on the sacramental question, "What does the sign say?" It is consonant with the method described in Chapter Two, where sacramental theologians begin with a phenomenological analysis of each human situation to which the individual sacraments correspond, and of each ritual sign. Out of that analysis, they draw insights and conclusions about the sacrament's meaning. Out of a similar analysis of Jesus' words and deeds as the Gospels present them, Christologists have come to a renewed appreciation of his self-identity as the historical sign of the presence of God.

Another Christological starting point accords well with current directions in sacramental theology. Classical western thought has focused largely on Jesus' role in humankind's redemption from sin. Christological questions about his person flow naturally into soteriological questions about his purpose. This largely medieval and post-medieval approach has been characterized as a "remedial" theology because it looks backwards to Jesus' place in repairing the damage done in and to the world because of Adam's sin. It is a valid but partial approach, because it ignores the strain in biblical documents like Romans, Colossians, and Ephesians, and Patristic writers like Irenaeus. These sources view the person and role of Jesus as oriented toward the future. Drawing on their richness, some thinkers today emphasize Jesus' place in the fulfilment of the cosmos. Among others, Pierre Teilhard de Chardin and Karl Rahner hold that Jesus Christ has to do not only with remedying the beginnings of our world and the enduring effects of original sin in our world.[1] He also has to do with that world's end or goal. Ultimately, that end or goal is the "restoration of all things in Christ," the complete fulfilment of that world with God. Out of a similar perspective, theologians view sacraments not only as related to our sinful condition, not only as remedies for human weakness. They are with equal if not greater importance, proleptic signs of God's fulfilling presence in human history, hints of the presence that we experience "already, but not yet," intimations of the future time when all tears will be wiped away, and God will truly be All in All. Using simple created things like water, wine, oil, words, and people, sacraments manifest the promise inherent in the whole created order.

---

[1]See Pierre Teilhard de Chardin, *The Divine Milieu* (New York: Harper and Row, 1960), *Hymn of the Universe* (New York: Harper and Row, 1965), and Karl Rahner, "Christology within an Evolutionary View of the World," *Theological Investigations V* (Baltimore: Helicon Press, 1966), pp. 157-192.

B. THE SACRAMENTAL SIGNIFICANCE OF TRADITIONAL CHRISTOLOGICAL DOCTRINES

Two classical doctrines regarding the person of Christ (Incarnation), his own fulfilment and permanent mode of presence (death-resurrection) provide the basic framework for this chapter. We seek the insights that these faith-convictions yield for our understanding of the sacraments. What and how does each contribute? To answer this question, we shall examine the structure of each doctrine.

1. The structure of the Incarnation

In Chalcedon's definition that the same Lord Jesus Christ is "perfect in divinity and perfect in humanity, the same truly God and truly man ... the same one in being with the Father as to the divinity and one in being with us as to the humanity,"[2] the church affirms the double-edged focus of the Incarnation. Approaching this doctrine from the perspective of our interests, many theologians today explore the reality of Jesus Christ as the great sign of God. This is the "sacramental" import of his divinity. With equal truth, he is the great sign of the faithful human response to God. This is the "sacramental" import of his humanity. While the significance of Christ's divinity has received the bulk of classical Christology's attention (sometimes bordering on a dangerous monophysitism), the significance of his humanity (aided by the Synoptic methodology discussed above) has received renewed attention in our time.

Sources for reflection on the sacramental implications of the Incarnation include the prologue to the Gospel according to John (John 1:1-18). While many earlier theologians used this text as a primary referent for a Logos, descent-Christology, it can also function as a source for a Christology and a sacramentology "from below." To this passage

---

[2]J. Neuner and J. Dupuis, eds. *The Christian Faith* (New York: Alba House, 1981), p. 154, Item 614.

today, theologians can bring the phenomenological understanding of symbol discussed in Chapters Two and Three. In
this view, symbolic language and activity both reveal and
conceal, express but do not exhaust the reality of which they
are a sign. Such language and activity are eminently suited
both to human and divine communication. Therefore, they
are eminently appropriate to that "admirable exchange," the
Incarnation.

John 1:1-18 is a rich resource for theological reflection.
This includes reflection that would serve our interests. While
considerable debate surrounds the question of the techni-
cally sacramental content of John's Gospel, there is little
debate over this Gospel's preoccupation with signs and with
Jesus as sign.[3] The primary sensory image is visual, since the
Gospel is about seeing. The kind of seeing entailed is both a
revealing and concealing, a disclosure and veiling at the
same time.

The prologue contains numerous themes which enter early
into the tradition of sacramental symbolism. "In the beginning" (John 1:1) recalls the motifs of creation and the covenant into which God entered with humankind as far back as
its beginnings (Genesis 1-3). The themes of creation, light,
and life become a strong triad of symbolic language, especially in the Fathers of the church. Augustine's definition of
sacraments as "visible words" builds on *Logos*, the primary
Christological title of this passage. Like the Word of God,
sacraments communicate. Like the Word, they are effective
signs because in them, as in that Word, God *does* what God
says.

Traditionally, verse 14 has received the bulk of theological
commentary. "And the Word became flesh and dwelt among
us, full of grace and truth." The verse remains prominent in
contemporary reflection. The Word became *flesh*, therefore
something or someone earthy and concrete. The Word of
God took on a human history. Therefore, God's concrete

---

[3]See Raymond Brown, "The Johannine Sacramentary," *New Testament Essays*
(Garden City, NY: Image Books, Doubleday, 1968), pp. 77-107.

sign and offer of salvation is not empty words, words, words. By assuming our human history, God's saving Word is no mere abstract instruction and exhortation, but ultimate involvement. Through human generation, God's Word walks the whole human journey, from the promise of birth to the finality of death. In the Word become flesh, in the created humanity of Jesus the Christ, we meet *the* definitive sign of God's presence and care for the world.

Karl Marx is reputed to have advised that, if you want an idea to catch on, you should wrap it up in a person. His political insight is surely in accord with the theological claim of John 1:14.

A chain of related concepts appears in and through the Prologue. Flesh = Word = Revelation/Communication = Sign. What is the content of this sign? On the one hand, Jesus Christ is the sign, revelation, or disclosure of who God is. And who is God? What did God do in history? The text hearkens back to Israelite tradition. The Hebrew God was the kind of deity who pitched a tent among people and wandered with them on their journeys. This God was no aloof clock-winder after the image of the eighteenth century deists. No, this God traveled and stayed with people — as mercy and fidelity, forgiveness and rock-like presence, grace and truth. The Greek text of John 1:14 echoes this Israelite terminology. The image behind "dwelt among us" is "pitched a tent among us," a clear reference to the Exodus tradition of the accompanying presence of God. The Greek words translated *grace* and *truth* are the equivalents of *hesed* and *'emet*, classical predicates of the Israelite God. Thus, verse 14 sets the direction for the rest of the Gospel. Those who truly see Jesus with the eyes of faith will see a sign of the merciful, faithful, pilgrim God.

This text deliberately employs terms from the category of covenant or relationship. The remarks immediately above commented on the divine aspect of this covenant. Contemporary Christology explores with equal vigor the other side, the human side. Not only does the Incarnation reveal God's presence in history. Not only is the Word made flesh a sign of God. The Incarnation is also a disclosure, a sign of the faithful human response to that God. Not only does the Incarnation manifest God's enduring, merciful care. The concrete, earthy, fleshly existence of God's Word reveals a man who worships God as creature. Jesus Christ is the perfect human response to the ever-caring, ever-present God.

The structure of the Incarnation is the twofold direction of God to humankind and of humankind to God. It is the structure of covenant. Covenant is also the structure of sacraments. Sacraments are the visible enactment of both sides of the relationship between God and humankind. In Jesus Christ, we see the mystery both of God's offer of salvation and of the human response to that offer. In the sacraments, God offers a mode of presence (welcoming, feeding, healing, calling to commitment . . .) and the people respond in grateful worship.

Vatican II's ritual renewal highlights the visibility of this covenant structure in each sacrament. After the introductory prayers, each celebration begins with biblical readings and a homily. This structure is the normal or standard practice. It expresses the truth that, in each sacrament as in our whole religious existence, God speaks first to the community assembled, and to humankind. Only after it hears God's Word does the community respond to that Word through a ritual action. The exchange of wedding vows, the laying on of hands, anointing of the sick, breaking and sharing of bread: all take place after the faithful have listened to God's Word. This word-action framework is a clear example, not only of the covenant-structure of the Incarnation and of sacraments. It expresses the very structure of the foundations of our Christian faith. We do not initiate our own salvation. That is, we do not act and in so acting save ourselves. The bedrock conviction of our Judeo-Christian tradition is that God first speaks and acts, and we respond in grateful commitment. In this sense, every sacrament is a *eucharistia*, an event of thankful response.

Implications of the incarnational structure of sacraments are far-reaching, and go beyond strictly sacramental issues.

In the Incarnation, God is not against humankind. God is
and acts for humankind, in and through its concrete history.
In the Incarnation, the divinity of Jesus is not in competition
with his humanity. Divinity and humanity do not co-exist in
inverse proportion to one another. Rather, the mystery of
the Incarnation lies precisely in the fact that, the more Jesus
Christ is divine, the more he is human. By logical extension,
salvation is not "in spite of," but "in and through and in the
midst of" human experience. Religion and sacraments are
not denials of human experience. Because God's Word really
did become flesh, we continue to meet and recognize that
Word in the familiar moments of human life — birth, reconciliation, hunger, sickness, commitment.

We owe much to Edward Schillebeeckx and to Karl
Rahner for their recovery of the notion that Jesus Christ is
both the great, primordial sacrament of God and of human
fidelity to that same God. We owe much to their insistence
that Jesus Christ becomes expressed in history especially in
and through the church. In and through the sacrament
which is the church, we have the particular, individual sacraments. In each, the church prolongs and renders palpable
the presence and saving actions of the Word made flesh.

2. The structure of death-resurrection

a. Gospel proclamations

After the death of Jesus, the first "doctrine" or faith-
statement of his followers was a dim but growing awareness
of his resurrrection. Following on this initial awareness, the
church as an enduring community and sacraments as enduring rituals became an issue. Why? Jesus' earthly, historical
life had ended in his death. His followers no longer enjoyed
his physical presence. But, coming out of the shock of the
crucifixion, they lived with the growing conviction that he
was still with them. Where? and how?

These and related questions form the background context
for several New Testament passages. In the Gospel according to John, Chapters 20 and 21 are a paradigm of the

numerous ways in which those who had known and loved Jesus of Nazareth continued to experience him as risen Lord. He was present in individual testimonies of faith (20:1-18, 24-29); in the community assembled and in forgiveness of sins (20:19-23); in meals together (21:1-14); in pastoral authority (21:15-19); in witness (20:30-31 and 21:24-25); and in the ongoing journey of faith (21:20-23). The Emmaus story (Luke 24:13-35) affirms his presence in the perplexity of his followers, in the Word proclaimed, in friendship with a stranger and, most dramatically, in the breaking and sharing of bread.

In the resurrection proclamation of the Synoptic Gospels, we receive a clue as to how the early followers interpreted their experience. In the earliest Gospel, Mark 16:1-8 is an important text. Verse 6 provides the structure of the community's experience of Jesus' death-resurrection. The young man at the tomb states, "You seek Jesus of Nazareth. He has been raised. He is not here." Whenever the Gospel writers speak of Jesus of Nazareth, they are referring to the physical Jesus of history, not the proclaimed Christ of faith. By using his earthly name, this text affirms a continuity with that person. But it also affirms a transformation in his mode of being. The negative expression of this transformation is "He is not here." And why is he not here? The positive but mysterious formulation tells us, "He has been raised." This cryptic verse affirms that the same person whom the faithful women had known continues to live, but in a new and transformed way. The structure of the biblical proclamation of death-resurrection is a structure of continuity-transformation.

While this structure is basic to the early Christians' affirmation of faith, it is not the beginning and end of the story. Assent to this claim demands a response — the imperative of active commitment and involvement in the proclamation (16:7, 15, 20 — go, tell, preach); the conversion from unbelief to belief (16:11, 13, 14). Gradually, the followers of Jesus continued to live with the conviction that this same man of Nazareth was still with them, but in a totally new way as Christ, as Lord. While they continued to know his presence in all the ways enumerated above, they put special emphasis on the moments when they gathered for worship — the baptismal initiation, and their regular breaking of bread in the Lord's Supper. They saw these as "focused moments" of the risen Lord's presence and action in their midst.

The structure of this death-resurrection proclamation becomes the structure of Christian sacramental experience. In these events of communal worship, the same person continues to do what he did on earth — good and saving actions that proclaimed the reign of God. Healing, calling to service and discipleship, restoring to community, feeding the hungry: these and other "saving moments" continue Christ's ongoing life in the church.

b. Resurrection appearances

Much debate revolves around the historicity and purpose of the appearance narratives in the Gospels. These are the stories that follow the initial proclamation that Jesus has been raised. While resolution of the debate exceeds the scope of this volume, we can make some judgments regarding the theological purpose of these accounts. Their role and function is to serve as a transition from the disciples' experience of the earthly Jesus to their experience of the glorified Lord. Jesus is no longer "there" among them, to be looked at and known in an empirical, physically tangible way. While the *noli me tangere* (do not touch me) has appeared in more exhortations to celibacy than one can count, its real meaning is "Do not hold me" or, more precisely, "Do not (try to) hold me back." Jesus no longer exists in his former way. Therefore, his followers can no longer know him in that former way.

These stories illustrate the community's new ways of experiencing their old leader Jesus of Nazareth, now their risen Lord. Analysis of these human encounters reveals that the Lord and his disciples meet one another in life-giving and life-demanding moments. After his earthly life and tragic death, the way in which Jesus is alive (risen) affects the way in which the community can experience him. That way is only in and through human situations, human interaction, human signs. And "he was known to them in the breaking of the bread" (Luke 24:35).

A new element is necessary for those who would continue to know this man Jesus. Though it took a kind of faith to walk with Jesus in his earthly life, it took no faith to see him, hear him, know his family. He was "there," walking the dusty roads of Galilee, available. But in his risen state, the element of religious faith is necessary. We have no record of cool, objective, outside observers meeting the risen Lord. By the very fact that he rejoined the disciples, even Thomas was predisposed to faith (John 20:24-29). If faith is a necessary element in the community's experience of its Lord, it is an equally necessary ingredient in every sacramental action. Bread looks like bread. And it is. But it is more. Wine tastes like wine. And it is. But it is more. Like all sacraments, the Eucharist is truly a "mystery of faith." Like the death-resurrection of Jesus, these symbolic actions make no sense at all to those who, at least on a minimal level, do not believe.

The principal theme underlying these appearance stories is the presence of the risen Christ. Biblical authors do not attempt a technical explanation of the mode of this presence. They are content with examples or illustrations of it. Some later Scholastic theologians spent a great deal of energy discussing and debating the "how" of Christ's acting presence in church and sacraments. The Aristotelian category of causality provided a favorite linchpin for their clarifying efforts. But none totally succeeded in pinning the matter down. The earlier Fathers of the Church were more guarded in their theologizing. None attempted a precise, technical treatment of the mode of Christ's enduring presence. They came closest when speaking of the Spirit as the living memory of Christ's living presence in the church. Such language leaves a great deal "open" regarding the manner of Christ's ecclesial and sacramental presence. It is in the spirit of the later medieval theologian Aquinas, whose basic answer to the "how" of his presence was "through the mysterious power of Christ."

Again, language like that leaves a great deal of latitude for ongoing exploration.

There is one further aspect of Christ's ecclesial and sacramental presence that bears noting. The presence of the risen Christ does not remove the simultaneous fact of his absence. In the church and in its sacraments, the risen Lord is already among us though not fully experienced. In biblical imagery, he is here as seed, as downpayment. In theological language, his presence is eschatological.

This insight into the experienced but not fulfilled character of Christ's risen presence has important practical consequences. Those who take it seriously will not seek an unrealistic religious "high" from each and every sacramental event. They will not absolutize any single ecclesial or sacramental experience. They will view celebrations of initiation, magnificent as they might be, as shadows of the final welcome that awaits us in the arms of God. They will view the Eucharist as a *taste* of the joyful satisfaction that we shall know fully at the heavenly banquet. They will approach the emotion-laden moments of marriage or ordination within the perspective of the "everyday," ordinary demands that these commitments will make on those who enter into them.

c. The meaning and results of the resurrection

The Gospels give us the structure of the resurrection-proclamation and specific instances of the ways in which the earliest Christian communities knew their risen Lord. The letters of Paul develop the meaning and results of the resurrection. Paul was an evangelist *par excellence*. Therefore, the bulk of his writing is geared toward proclaiming a persuasive message which would result in initiation, in new members entering into the life and mission of the risen Lord. In so many of his letters. Paul elaborates on the general theme, "As Christ, so we." This pattern informs what is probably the earliest account of Jesus' death-resurrection, that found in I Corinthians 15. In this important passage, Paul is not simply offering his own opinions. He is handing on what he has received as tradition. As he enters actively into the handing-on process, he interprets and clarifies the meaning of the death-resurrection event.

"He was raised"(I Cor 15:4). So shall we be. For Paul, what happened to Jesus will happen to us. What did happen? In their post-apologetic stance toward the resurrection, recent theologians have approached this question out of a Christology "from below." In the resurrection, Jesus did not "prove" that he was God. Rather, in this event, God fully communicated God's own self and God's own power to the Son (Romans 1:3-4). The result was not proof of Jesus' divinity, but fulfilment of his humanity. The resurrection was a manifestation of what had happened in Jesus' entire self-giving life, a life that climaxed in his death. Throughout his lifetime, Jesus had handed himself over to the mysterious mission of a merciful, loving God. The ultimate handing-over occurred on the cross. God accepted that handing-over. This acceptance issued forth in new and continuing life. We call that life "resurrection." The Pauline texts that posit the link between the resurrection of Jesus and the resurrection begun in and promised to his followers are too numerous to enumerate. But the familiar passages about death to life in Colossians (2:12ff.) and Ephesians (2:1-7) complement the message of I Corinthians 15.

In his theology, Paul not only links Jesus' raised humanity with that of other humans, namely his faithful followers. Paul links Jesus' risen existence with the whole creation. Freed from the limits of space and time, Jesus now enjoys unrestricted presence to the world. The risen Lord not only becomes the firstborn of all humanity (Colossians 1). He becomes the hope of groaning creation (Romans 8). The transformation of this creature is the beginning and promise of transformation for the whole created order, the sign of what is to come for all. In Jesus' self-gift and God's loving acceptance of that gift, a part of our world became so given over to God in trustful love, that that part continues to live in our world, transformed and transforming.

The resurrection is God's "Yes," God's acceptance of the whole human life that Jesus had lived. It is God's answer to the whole spectrum of his human fidelity. The sequence of events is very instructive. God speaks this "Yes" in and through Jesus' death, not around or in spite of it. This God is author of life, to be sure, but a life that cannot come to be without a prior dying. "Unless a grain of wheat falls into the earth and dies, it remains alone; but if it dies, it bears much fruit" (John 12:24). We cannot reach Easter except by going through Good Friday. We cannot sing "Alleluia" without first lamenting "Why have you forgotten me?"

I Corinthians 15:45 most directly presents the results of Jesus' resurrection for us. Jesus Christ is not just alive, as if Easter Sunday were his private reward for a faithful Good Friday. According to Paul, he is "life-giving spirit." As such, he continues to do what he had done on earth — to bring light to the blind, strength to the lame, hope to the hopeless ... He does this not simply by his own actions, but by empowering his followers to do the same. They are the ones to preach God's Word, to confront, to reconcile, to call to service (see Mt. 28:19; Lk 24:49; John 20:21). "As Christ, so we."

Every sacrament incarnates the structure of Jesus' death-resurrection. In faith, we affirm that the same Jesus of Nazareth continues to live and act among us in a new way. Each sacrament issues a call to die to something, in order to live in Christ. We are called to die to sin in baptism and reconciliation, in order to live well in Christ and with one another. We are called to die to debilitating fear in anointing, in order to live in hope. We are called to die to our own self-enclosed worlds in marriage and orders, in order to live in the larger world of family and service to the church. We are called to die to selfishness in the Eucharist, in order to break open our lives to the people for whom Christ gave his.

The resurrection of Jesus provides and demands a movement into ecclesiology. The Spirit of God is the dynamic presence behind this movement. The Spirit is the bond between God and Jesus as risen Lord (Romans 1:3-4), the risen Lord and the church (Romans 8:9-11) and, finally, the church and its sacramental life. The Spirit is the "missing link" in sacramental theology, the power that continues Christ's presence and mission throughout the whole life of the church, including its liturgical worship. The same Spirit that animates creation and human history animates the symbolic actions of the people of God. The ritual prayers that invoke God's Spirit give witness to this belief.

Continuing our descriptive definitions of sacraments from various perspectives, we can say that sacraments are the risen Christ's saving activity in its historical, visible availability to us. The man Jesus received and experienced the fulness of God's love in his own resurrection. In the sacramental acts of a believing community, he makes himself and that love historically available to us. Thus, we remain in continuity with him.

Sacraments are not the continuation of Jesus *as he was.* In some late medieval thought and practice this truth was forgotten, and bizarre stories of Jesus' blood dripping if one chewed the Host circulated, even down to recent times. Cadavers on the altar "represented" the physical body of Christ. But sacraments are signs not of the physical, but of the risen Christ. They are the earthly prolongation of Christ's transformed, glorified humanity. Therefore, they should transform the lives of those who participate in them. They should not leave us *as we were.* "As Christ, so we." In Jesus' self-gift on the cross, he confronted and conquered the ultimate human fear, death itself. His resurrection showed that death is not, nor will it be God's last word. Hope is engendered out of, not in spite of death. Transformation from death to life and despair to hope becomes a mode of revelation. It tells us who God is, and what God is about in human history.

This emphasis on transformation is extremely important, if a sacramental religion is not simply to be a palliative for pain or an excuse for inaction. Neither Jesus' resurrection nor sacraments eliminate death and sin. But in them, death becomes transformed. Death wears many faces. There are the personal traits in each of us that must die if we are to live faithfully in Christ. There are the interpersonal relationships that need to be transformed if we are to be life-giving for one another. And in our time, we recognize a sober fact. There are the institutionalized, structural forms of oppression that must die if men and women are to live as free, dignified children of God. Transformation does not happen automatically, as if wishing could make it so. It demands an entering into death — to sin, to selfishness, to fear of institutional reprisal, if "new life" is to mean anything more than a pious slogan.

In our eschatological time, this time between his first and final coming, Jesus Christ does not show himself to his followers in his own flesh. He makes himself available only by taking up earthly, non-glorified realities like bread and wine, water and people, into his saving activity. In his church and its sacraments, Jesus continues to use human things, events, words, and actions as God had used his own earthly life: to proclaim new possibilities for all people in and through the coming of the reign of God. In and through the human sign that is the church, God's mission in Christ would go on. In and through the symbolic activities of that community, created realities would continue to "bring to light" the scope and meaning of that mission.

3. Suffering

While this chapter has focused on linking Christian sacraments with the Incarnation and death-resurrection of Jesus, discussion of the latter has really centered on the resurrection aspect of this belief. It is appropriate to examine the meaning of Jesus from yet another angle, that of the problem of suffering. This is theologically necessary, not only because Jesus clearly suffered during the course of his lifetime and in the culminating event of his death. It is theologically and anthropologically necessary because of the enormity of suffering in human history. Holocausts of all kinds, senseless terrorism, a child struck with leukemia, drought threatening an entire continent: all give poignant testimony to this fact of suffering. "As Christ, so we." Followers of Christ claim a link between the meaning of his suffering and their own. This link is not simply a pious placebo to help them to endure. That would be unworthy of their human dignity, an insult to their intelligence. If their life is like that of Christ, then it must be critically aware and self-transcending. Therefore, Christians are obliged to search out the meaning of suffering and to allow their own suffering to inform and transform the way they think and feel. The goal of this thinking and feeling is not self-pity or self-induction into the order of martyrs. Rather, it is to enable believers to become more sensitive to the truth of the human situation, and more attuned to the truth that faith brings to that situation.

In every age, thinkers have grappled with the problems of theodicy. Traditionally, theodicy has explored philosophical proofs for the existence of God and the enduring human question, "Why suffering, why evil?" Today, theodicy approaches the latter theme not primarily by "justifying" the co-existence of human suffering and an all-powerful, good God. Rather, it explores the problem of evil in relation to the image of a vulnerable God. This image has firm though often neglected roots in our Judeo-Christian tradition. Isaiah describes this vulnerable God: "For he said, 'Surely they are my people' . . . and he became their Savior. In all their affliction he was afflicted, and the angel of his presence saved them" (Isaiah 63:8-9). In the Isaian servant songs (Is 42:1-4; 49:1-6; 50:4-9; 52:13-53: 12), the image is transposed to the servant of God, an individual or a people who acts on God's behalf, as a light to the nations (Is. 49:6). What kind of light does this figure shed? It is a light that sees human suffering not primarily as a consequence of human sinfulness, though this theme does appear elsewhere in the Scriptures (e.g., Job 3:7-9; John 9:2). But here, the light of the Servant's suffering primarily reveals God's redemptive power.[4]

It is little wonder that the early Christians turned to those texts in their Israelite tradition which echoed and affirmed

---

[4]This theme stands in marked contrast to many other Old Testament texts which come out of a monarchical period and, therefore, image a monarchical God.

this vulnerability theme. After all, they had to justify to themselves the ignominious death of the one they had followed, the man in whom they had put their hopes. No wonder they borrowed so freely from the servant songs, in the Gospels and Acts. These texts not only "explained" the suffering messiah. These passages led them back, ultimately, to the kind of God who not only walked with, but suffered with people. In Christ the crucified, they re-met their suffering God. A recent address speaks eloquently to this point:

> It is not sheer power but the vulnerability of suffering love that inspires us. It is through the cross of Christ that we learn who God is. It is the cross that finally breaks our old monarchical image of God. It is the cross that clearly provides us with a new image: an image of a vulnerable God, an image of a crucified God, an image of a God who redeems us not by coercive power but by suffering with us in our suffering.[5]

In the enthusiasm of Vatican II, many turned to a theology and spirituality based largely, if not exclusively, on the joy of the resurrection. "We are Easter people, and *Alleluia* is our song." While this might have been a natural reaction to an overly Passion-centered, overly ascetic Christian practice, it was equally one-sided, at least in those versions which downplayed the *death*-resurrection unity. Twenty years after the Council, believers are pondering with renewed interest the meaning and power of the cross. The traditional link between cross and resurrection remains prominent. Thus, the theology of the cross reveals to us that in our darkness, including the darkness of death, God will meet us. Precisely in this void of non-being, human beings meet the re-creative power of God.

In current thinking on the theology of the cross, a new

---

[5]Burton Z. Cooper, "Why, God? A Tale of Two Sufferers," *Convocation Address* at Louisville Presbyterian Theological Seminary (Sept. 4, 1984), p. 14. Privately circulated.

theme has emerged. This theme links and explicitates the relationship between suffering and the first doctrine examined in this chapter, Incarnation. The theology of the cross is first of all a witness to the Incarnation. It is a way of speaking about God's entry into the sphere of human history and, therefore, a revelation of the kind of God worthy of human trust. This God is Emmanuel, God-with-us. And where is God-with-us? Recognition of the unity between cross and Incarnation answers clearly. Do not look to the sky and the stars, do not look first to glory for God. Look to Emmanuel, the one made flesh, the one who has been crucified. For the physical body of Christ, crucifixion was a one-time event. For his mystical body and for the whole body of humankind, crucifixion is a never-ending possibility. If the church prolongs the Incarnation and if Emmanuel *remains* God-with-us, then we meet this kind of God wherever we meet suffering humanity. In the personal suffering of individuals and in the communal suffering of whole peoples, we meet the human face (sign, revelation, disclosure ...) of God.

Every sacrament addresses, in some way, the reality of human suffering. Baptism launches one on a journey of continual conversion, and such "turning" is alway painful. Marriage calls for mutual commitment" in good times and in bad, for better or for worse." Orders requires a submission of one's personal wants, needs, and choices to the pastoral needs of the church. This structuring of suffering into sacraments is not only because life is bittersweet so that, if they are to be faithful expressions of that life, sacraments must never dissolve the bittersweet tension. It is also because in the sacraments we encounter the God of Jesus Christ, a God whose primary attribute is not overwhelming power, but suffering love. The Incarnation teaches us that God is most present, most with us, at the weak spots of the world. Jesus' invitation to Thomas remains relevant for all time. "Touch my wounds," the wounds of men, women, and children everywhere. The wounds of humankind are the enduring sacrament, the continuing sign, of the Incarnation. "My Lord and my God" (John 20:28).

III. Supportive readings

The starting-point for current thinking on the Christological foundations of sacraments is the sacramental nature of Christ himself. The category of *revelation*, as discussed in Chapter Three, remains important here.

—Cooke, Bernard. *Sacraments and Sacramentality* (Mystic, CT: Twenty-Third Publications, 1983), pp. 56-67.

> "What did Jesus do that has changed the meaning of our human reality?" In his treatment of Christ's institution of sacraments, Cooke sees Jesus' living, dying, and rising as transforming "the reality and significance of what it means to be human." Such transformation is a new revelation from God. Cooke links the broad themes of symbolic signs, revelation, resurrection, and transformation to the often narrow question, "Did Christ institute the sacraments?"

—Osborne, Kenan. "Methodology and the Christian Sacraments." *Worship* 48 (1974), pp. 536-549 and "Jesus as Human Expression of the Divine Presence." In Francis Eigo, ed. *The Sacraments: God's Love and Mercy Actualized* (Philadelphia: Villanova University Press, 1979), pp. 29-57.

> Among North American theologians, Osborne has written most academically and most extensively on the relation between Jesus Christ and the sacraments. His 1974 article suggests and links two methodological approaches to sacraments, the anthropological and the Christological. He explores the important principle that sacraments (signs) are always *of* something, *for* someone(s), and the significance of this principle for sacramental understanding.
>
> The purpose of his 1979 article is to show the insufficiency of the Scholastic definition of sacraments, and to call for a new understanding. Because the nature of symbols is both to reveal and conceal at the same time, sacraments are not static

but dynamic, not reified but processive. ". . . the very *wholeness* of being human, bodily and spiritual, manifest and concealed, is the locus of the primordial sacramentality of Jesus."

Osborne is unabashedly philosophical, building largely on phenomenologists like Merleau-Ponty. His scholarly, technical articles are well worth the effort.

—Vaillancourt, Raymond. *Toward a Renewal of Sacramental Theology* (Collegeville, Minn.: The Liturgical Press, 1979), pp. 36-40, 88-90.

Vaillancourt gives a brief but clear explanation of how Jesus Christ is an "actant" in the sacraments. Building on the fact that God has always acted through intermediaries, he discusses the sacramental nature of every activity of Christ. Thus, he too broadens the "institution" question.

5

Ecclesiological Foundations of Sacramental Action

I. Orienting questions and readings

A. The following technical terms occur in classical sacramental theology. What do they mean? What issues and problems are associated with each?

— ex opere operato
— ex opere operantis
— causality
— validity

B. "Sacraments are acts of the church." In what sense do you understand this statement? What is the relationship between the Roman Catholic church and its sevenfold sacramental system?

"The church is a sacrament." In what sense do you understand this statement? How does it relate to the concepts discussed in Chapters One to Four?

C. Read J. Neuner and J. Dupuis, eds., "The Sacraments of the Church," *The Christian Faith* (New York: Alba House, 1981), pp. 365-381. In order to avoid a fundamentalist distortion and to gain a full appreciation of their meaning, these official teachings should be read with a knowledge of their historical, political, and religious context. However, for purposes of an overview of sacramental doctrine, even a reading of these formal statements in isolation from their contexts is instructive. Read this chapter, noting what themes or issues recur in official sacramental teaching. What do the statements say? What do they not say?

II. Reflections

A. THE SPIRIT OF CHRIST

"As Christ, so we." This Pauline theme expresses the natural and dynamic relationship between Christology and ecclesiology. The same Spirit of God who animated Jesus of Nazareth in his historical life and resurrection animates his life as risen Lord in the church. The same power who incarnated God in Jesus Christ still incarnates the presence of God in the lives of Jesus' followers. A biblical perspective does not allow too ethereal a view of the Spirit of God. Throughout our Judeo-Christian texts and tradition, the Spirit acts concretely, in people and events that make a difference in human history. The Spirit does not act alone, but in and through people "seized" by God's power and driven by God's mission. As the church's *living* memory, the Spirit links Christians through the ages to their living Lord. This linkage receives concrete expression in and through the symbolic actions of the church, its sacraments.

B. THE CHURCH AS SACRAMENT

Chapter One noted that one of the earliest Christian usages of *mysterion (sacramentum)* occurred in the letters to Colossians and the Ephesians. In these texts, the primary referent for the term was the church, that community which is the focus of God's saving plan as that plan operates in human, communal, and historically recognizable form. From Christ, the church itself has a sacramental structure because it continues his life and work in and through its human signs.

Because of their canonical preoccupations and attention to individual sacraments, medieval theologians allowed this biblical and patristic image of church as sacrament to recede into the shadows. It remained dormant for many years. While Vatican II did not employ this image as its dominant description of the church's self-identity, the council did allow it to re-emerge. "By her relationship with Christ, the Church is a kind of sacrament or sign of intimate union with God, and of the unity of all mankind" (*Dogmatic Constitution on the Church*, Art. 1). The image develops in two directions. First, the church is the sacrament of the risen Christ — the expression, in historical and eschatological form, of Christ's saving actions and ultimate victory over sin and death. It is not only the continuation of the risen Christ's saving presence. Ever dynamic, the church is the sign of Christ's ongoing mission in the world: proclaiming the reign of God, calling people to conversion and discipleship, breaking bondage of all kinds. In its very structure, each sacrament expresses its link with Christ. The ritual prayers express what he achieved in the past "for us and for our salvation," what his mediating grace continues to do in the present, and what believers must hope and strive for until he comes in future final glory. Like Christ, his church is the sign of God's work in the world, already begun and yet to be brought to completion.

In a second line of development, the council views the church as a sacrament of the salvation of the world. On a pastoral and ecumenical level, this direction of thought is extremely important. In this vein, the church expresses its self-definition not as over against the world, not in terms of *its* sole possession of power, holiness, and truth. Rather, this community identifies itself in terms of its ability to be a sign.

By creation and even more explicitly by the Word's Incarnation, God took the world seriously and fundamentally into the dynamic of saving mercy. The vocation of all people is to be with God. By becoming one with human history through the Incarnation, God consecrated humanity. The one "who desires all to be saved and to come to the knowledge of the truth" (I Tim. 2:4) *hopes* salvation for humankind.

This universalist thrust does not deny the Judeo-Christian theme of election. But the "elect" are not those who are saved in contrast to others. The elect are those chosen to bear God's good news to others. Election is both a gift and a responsibility. Most important, election does not equal exclusive possession. To be elect is to be a sign — partial but powerful, light-bearing but limited. Thus, the church of Christ is a sacrament, an explicit sign of what God hopes and intends for all people. This community is a kind of "official" presence of God's grace in Christ, in the public history of the human race. When it responds faithfully to its call, it is the abiding promulgation of Christ's grace-giving presence to the world. In the name of the race, the church of Christ is that segment of humankind which responds consciously to God's initiative in the world.

While Roman Catholics today take this stance of institutional modesty for granted, its initial impact was revolutionary. In a classic volume on Christian self-understanding, Karl Rahner captures the sharp contrast between a pre-conciliar and conciliar attitude.

> For Christendom in earlier times the Church was the plank of salvation in the shipwreck of the world, the small barque on which alone men are saved, the small band of those who are saved by the miracle of grace from the *massa damnata*, and the *extra ecclesiam nulla salus* was understood in a very exclusive and pessimistic sense. But here in the conciliar text the Church is not the society of those who alone are saved, but the sign of the salvation of those who, as far as its historical and social structure are concerned, do not belong to it. By their profession of faith, their worship and life, the

human beings in the Church form as it were the one expression in which the hidden grace promised and offered to the whole world emerges from the abysses of the human soul into the domain of history and society. What is there expressed may fall on deaf ears and obdurate heart in the individual and may bring judgment instead of salvation. But it is the sign of grace which brings what it expresses, and not only in cases where it is heard in such a way that the hearer himself visibly and historically joins the band of those who announce and testify to this word of God to the world. The Church is the sacrament of the salvation of the world even where the latter is still not and perhaps never will be the Church. It is the tangible, historical manifestation of the grace in which God communicates himself as absolutely present, close and forgiving, of the grace which is at work everywhere, omits no one, offers God to each and gives to every reality in the world a secret purposeful orientation towards the intrinsic glory of God.[1]

Rahner's formulation brings together themes discussed earlier in this volume. If grace is God's self-revelation offered always and everywhere to all people in the depths of their existence, then the church is indeed a partial, though powerful expression of that offer. The church is not the exclusive possessor of the mystery of God. Rather, it is the sign and servant of that mystery.

Several corollaries flow from viewing the church as a sacrament deriving from the primordial sign of God, Jesus Christ. First, the institution of each sacrament as such is ecclesial, insofar as each expresses a particular dimension of the larger sign - character of the entire church. Sacraments are not the isolated acts of individual ministers or participants. They are symbolic activities which express and belong to the entire people of God. "The sacraments make the church, and the church makes the sacraments." Out of this

---

[1]Karl Rahner, *The Christian of the Future* (New York: Herder and Herder, 1968), pp. 82-83.

perspective, to speak of "Father's Mass" is to utter (or at least to border on) heresy. Primacy goes not to a single minister or believer, but to an assembly. The church is not only the place of, but the principal agent in sacramental celebrations.

This insight into the entire church as sacrament expresses the necessary unity between the church's liturgical and pastoral life. In its liturgical revisions, Vatican II integrated the church's rites into the great sign which is its whole life. This is both a danger and a challenge. Ritual acquires meaning only to the extent that it is sustained by and leads to pastoral action. Thus, the *Rite of Christian Initiation of Adults* is much more than water poured on new converts to the true faith. It is a process of communal welcoming, interaction, conversion, and support. Liturgical anointing makes no sense unless, in moments outside this ritual event, a parish or institution offers its healing presence to those who are sick.

The church's sacramental vocation is to carry on the work of God. This work, which is also the mission of Christ, belongs to all believers, at all moments. In its sevenfold expression, the church's sacramental system offers this "total package." Sacraments celebrate God's saving plan in each major life-situation. Conscious that the reality of sacrament comprises more than the ritual moment, the Catholic sacraments correspond to each major moment of human, communal experience. Entering and leaving a group, being nourished in its life, asking forgiveness, undergoing illness, and making commitments: these human events come to expression in the church's sacramental system.

Only recently have Catholics begun to reflect seriously on what it means to be a sacrament in a non-Christian society. U.S. political debates on abortion, birth control, and nuclear policy illustrate the struggle involved in maintaining a faith-commitment in a pluralistic milieu. Certainly, consciousness of one's identity as sacrament fosters a modesty with regard to one's claims, an awareness that persuasion must come about not through the coercive power of threat, but through the convincing power of sign. In its own life, of what is the church a sign? Only when its behavior clearly expresses the Gospel values it proclaims does the church's voice hold sway.

C. HISTORY OF SACRAMENTAL PRACTICE AND THOUGHT

Chapter One included a broad overview of developments in sacramental theology and practice, from the time of Jesus to recent times. Ecclesiological considerations require a highlighting of some of the more precise factors that have shaped the course of this community's life. Twentieth century theologians and practitioners have built on the historical and theological research of nineteenth century scholars like Johann Möhler and Matthias Scheeben. Their interest in biblical studies, the Eucharist, and ecclesiology has led to knowledge of the developmental nature of the church and, concomitantly, of sacraments. This view both contributed to and issued from Vatican II. A discussion of key insights emerging from this "historical consciousness" perspective follows.

While the New Testament makes reference to certain realities which the church later calls sacraments (e.g. marriage, anointing of the sick, official service), it does not use the term in a technical sense. The documents do give primary and direct attention to two ritual moments, baptism and the Lord's Supper. Both the bath and the meal are events of Christian initiation. Both are moments of forgiveness. Baptism initiates new members into a life of radical, ongoing conversion. The Lord's Supper sustains their life — nourishing, reconciling, calling to continual commitment. Both events accent the role of Christian believers in the community's mission. Neither suggests that membership promises complacency, much less an insurance of automatic salvation.

Theological development during the Patristic period

illustrates the principle that life precedes formulation, practice precedes theorizing. The Christian community lived its sacraments, and only subsequently reflected upon and regularized them. This was a period of cultural diversity and, therefore, of cultural adaptation. As the church expanded, it incorporated elements from both the Semitic and Hellenistic worlds into its initiation process. In the fourth century, Christianity gained state recognition and approbation. The influx of massive numbers of converts called forth new structures. The need for a period of serious and sustained formation in the faith resulted in the catechumenate. A period of prolonged and public penance was instituted for those who had seriously violated their baptismal commitment.

In its earliest years, the Christian community's worship and ministry were markedly desacralized. That is, there seemed to be a deliberate attempt to avoid or at least de-emphasize priestly and sacrificial nomenclature. With the church's official approbation and evangelistic expansion into northern Europe, the direction changed. Northern European tribes had long had an attraction for "holy places." This tendency became a natural base for the proliferation of Christian sanctuaries. Ministerial personnel and, especially, the Eucharist, took on priestly and sacrificial terminology. Levitical texts supported the growing practice, later mandated, of clerical continence.

Even with these developments, the notion of *sacrament* remained broad and varied for a long period of time. In the writings of Leo the Great for example (c. 400-461 A.D.), *sacrament* included the Christ-event, the church, the liturgical cycle, proclamation of the Gospel, ritual acts, the Eucharistic prayer of thanksgiving, and lives of the faithful. Only gradually did the Christian community's life-experience and theologizing on that experience lead to the reservation of this term for designated liturgical actions.

Two concrete pastoral questions led to a gradual clarifying of the concept, sacrament. The first had to do, ultimately, with the source of sacramental grace. Question: do the morals of a minister affect the reality, the validity of a sacrament? This theme emerged in numerous guises and contexts, as will be evident in the discussion on magisterial teaching below. The church's negative reply to the question introduced into sacramental theology a phrase that would be used and misused over the centuries. *Ex opere operato*: by the work having been done. The church's consistent reply was clear. By the work (the rite) having been done, *God's* power is at work. Therefore, the sacrament is real, valid, and effective. In its original usage, this technical formula in no way intended to foster a magical reliance on correct words, gestures, etc., as if they alone were the cause of sacramental grace. Rather, it intended to make clear that it is *God's* grace which is offered and assured through the official liturgical gestures of the church. While the minister's morals and manner might indeed negatively affect the quality of a celebration over which he presides, they do not block God's saving presence. God can and does work, even through flawed human instruments.

The second pastoral situation concerned the emergence of the concept of sacramental character. In practice, three sacraments were never repeated in an individual's life: baptism, confirmation, and orders. If a Christian "lapsed" from the faith and later wished to return to its practice, he or she was not re-baptized. If a minister left and later returned to his official service, he was not re-ordained. Under the pressure of controversy and the desire for clarification, the reason behind this practice of non-repeatability became articulated. Baptism, confirmation, and orders indicated an irrevocable relationship to the church. In baptism and confirmation, the relation was one of membership. During the Patristic period, a predominant image for initiation into the Christian community was that of new birth. Once a person was born physically, he or she was always a child of its parents. Even if parent or child rejected one another, the filial relationship could never really be broken. By analogy, the image applied to spiritual birth. No matter whether a Christian denied his or her baptism, that person remained a child of God. Therefore, if he or she wanted to return to Christian life, the baptismal (and confirmational) ritual was not repeated.

In the case of orders, the relation to the church was one of public leadership. Such leadership was so important for the community's life that it was viewed as an irrevocable commitment, both on the part of the ordained person and of God. Once a man entered into this relationship, it could never really be dissolved.

In medieval as well as in recent years, numerous studies have appeared on the nature of the sacramental character. Depending on the historical period or theologian in question, they demonstrate an astonishing variety in the understanding and "location" of sacramental character. There is a progression from the largely external focus of the Patristic period (*character* equals the sacramental rite itself or the visible effects of the rite, namely membership or service) to the medieval internal quality or mark on the soul. The core of the matter is most important. No matter the emphasis, sacramental character refers not so much to a "thing" as to a relationship. The reality should not be reified, as if character were a privileged possession. *Character* is a way of talking about mutual and ongoing commitment.

Chapter One discussed Augustine's principal contributions to sacramental theology, notably his early definitions of sacrament and his intent to maintain the effective unity between these symbolic signs and the realities they signified. This "signifying" emphasis dominated sacramental understanding for eight centuries, until the introduction of the next major category, that of sacramental causality. With its corollary notions of communication, instruction, and promise, this sign-aspect insisted that, to be truly fruitful in people's lives, sacramental actions involved their active, aware participation.

Not much explicit treatment of sacramental doctrine as such occurred from about the fifth to the eleventh centuries. During this period however, practical and portable aids were produced for the benefit of evangelizing missionaries. *Sacramentaries* provided standardized rituals. *Penitentiaries* included lists of sins with appropriate corresponding penances. While these types of books were useful, they had a negative side-effect. Especially when employed to the exclusion of other sacramental sources, they fostered a narrowing trend toward predominantly rubrical and canonical questions.

During this period, explicit issues emerged with regard to the validity of the sacraments. Under the influence of a growing "contrast" mentality as described in Chapter One, thinkers and practitioners began to envision a change in the relationship between the holy signs (sacraments) and the mystery they signified (an aspect of God's saving presence). They contrasted the outward form of the rites with the mystery that the rites intended to express. Especially as the Christian community moved more and more into Germanic areas, the conceptual unity between sign and reality was dissolved. It was a short and easy step toward an opposition and a dichotomous mentality. This attitude had detrimental effects, especially in the Eucharistic controversies of the early and late Middle Ages. The powerful sign-function of liturgical rites receded, paving the way toward an objectivist view of sacraments. These symbolic actions were viewed as an almost impersonal power, sources of grace established by divine ordination. The personal, communal, and symbolic dimensions of sacramental life began to fade into the background. The road to viewing sacraments as "things" was short and direct. Symbolism, and the intimate relationship between symbolic signs and reality was lost.

The Scholastic period (11th to 15th centuries) had great advantages and disadvantages, both connected with the increasing practice of sacramental clarification and codification. Collections of canon law, including the *Decree of Gratian*, became major sources for theological reflection. While this had practical value, it was accompanied by an allegorizing of biblical texts such that their primary meaning got submerged under the myriad details of interpretation. And loss of contact with many of the rich liturgical texts of the early church contributed to a "shrinking" in sacramental theology and practice.

Under Augustine's broad notion of *sacrament* as a sign of a sacred thing or event, in the twelfth century, marriage entered the realm of officially recognized sacraments. The incorporation of marriage into a grouping that included baptism and the Eucharist indicates that different criteria were applied in deciding which actions were and were not official sacraments. It is interesting to note that the inclusion of marriage as a "holy sign" corresponded to an unfortunate development in secular society. In some medieval circles, the contrast between matter and spirit was so strong that material reality, including the body, was looked down upon. In the face of this worldview, the church took a decidely countercultural turn when it affirmed the holiness of human love, as expressed through sexual intercourse.

This century also provides the first unequivocal enumeration of seven official sacraments in the technical sense. This occurs in the text often attributed to Peter Lombard, *Sententiae Divinitatis*. The listing is an explicit ratification of what had been implicitly accepted through practice. The later Councils of Florence (1431-37) and Trent (1545-63) did little more than transmit this listing. They neither attempted to examine it critically nor to justify it.

The appearance of a sevenfold sacramental system illustrates the principle of sacramental development noted above. The community's practice precedes the justifying rationale of its theologizing. And theologizing precedes the formalized acceptance of its official listing. Christians "lived" their sacraments long before they codified them.

Under the impact of a heightened historical consciousness, numerous scholars recently have asked the question, "Why seven?"[2] This question has ecumenical import, as well as import for an intelligent understanding of sacraments within our own Roman Catholic tradition. Though we can no

[2]See, for example, Christopher Kiesling, "How Many Sacraments?" *Worship* 44 (1970), pp. 268-276.

longer trace each sacrament directly back to a specific, intended institution in the life of Jesus, we can attempt an account of the origin of our sevenfold system, based on what thinkers of the Middle Ages would have viewed as "fitting." The Medieval mind had a penchant for order and symbolism. It saw in the number seven the symbol of fulness, completion, and balance. To theologians of the period, it was important that interior realities like vices, virtues, and even sacraments match the external structure of the cosmos. To their knowledge, the cosmos was composed of seven planets. These regulated the exterior world. Therefore, it was both logical and necessary that seven religious structures regulate the interior world. In addition to its popular association with fulness, the number seven had another symbolic value. It is a combination of the numbers three (symbol of the divine) and four (symbol of the human). How "fitting" then that seven official signs of the church signal both divine power and human response.

In its wisdom, the church of the Middle Ages canonized seven sacramental moments, symbolizing the plenitude of God's saving power offered to all human situations. Vatican II reaffirmed this insight, asserting the sacramental structure of the church's entire life and activity. That life and activity touch all the concrete situations of human life — birth and death, sustenance, healing, and commitment.

Reflection on the development of the sevenfold sacramental system illustrates another important point. Sacraments are truly ecclesial moments in the sense that the church determines those moments which are formally, officially sacrament. The seven rites become definitive moments with a privileged position in its liturgical life. They both express and shape this community of faith.

The thirteenth century contributed positively to the formulation of sacramental theory. Major theologians, especially Thomas Aquinas, incorporated the newly-discovered philosophical categories of Aristotle into their theological syntheses. These categories organized and gave theoretical intellectual foundations to what the Christian community had long believed and practiced. Aquinas adopted the distinctions of matter and form, substance and accidents, in explaining the structure of sacraments. In searching for a definition, he examined strains of thought implicit in Augustine and other early Fathers of the church. What is common to all the sacramental rites? In what category should sacraments be placed? Aquinas took up Augustine's traditional category of *sign*. By continuing to define sacraments as such, he continued to define these events in terms of meaning. He provided clarifications and narrowed in to a more technical definition by qualifying Augustine's idea that everything holy was a sacrament. He did so by introducing the category of causality into the definition of sacraments. Aquinas asserted that sacraments, in the narrower sense of the seven accepted rites, make something happen. *Significando causant*: they cause by signifying, or cause in accord with their power as signs. How? Explanations vary, both from Thomas and from other Scholastic theologians. The church never defines any of the explanations as requiring the assent of faith. What the church affirms, and what theologians agree upon, is that sacraments cause grace or bring about what they signify because God does what God says. We have a realization of what the signs intend to express, because God acts in and through them. The causality of a sacrament is co-extensive with and determined by its ritual sign. Only a correct and full reading of the sign can tell what is being caused. Thus, only a rich knowledge of the symbolism of water can lead to an awareness of what baptism causes. Only an insight into what happens when people eat together can convey the causality inherent in the Eucharistic meal.

In his theologizing, Aquinas makes extensive use of the principle of analogy. For example, as baptism is analogous to spiritual childhood, so confirmation is analogous to spiritual maturity. Informed by a more unified view of the sacraments of initiation, many theologians today reject this approach. But they will agree that arguments from fittingness and from analogy are legitimate forerunners of the "turn to the subject" which has so characterized contemporary theology.

Thomas Aquinas maintained a delicate balance between the categories of sign or meaning and causality or effectiveness. Unfortunately, many later Scholastics fell into an imbalance on the side of causality. This contributed to a static, mechanistic view of sacraments as "holy things." Proper matter and form insured an infallible result. A misunderstanding of the formula *ex opere operato* incurred the Reformers' valid critique that correct ritual performance, especially by the minister, left little room for the initiative of God. Having lost its liturgical and symbolic context, and having overemphasized the distinction between sign and reality, medieval sacramental theology became sterile and practice became perfunctory. Sacramental considerations gave primacy of place to institutional and hierarchical factors. The laity became spectators at a clerical celebration, recipients of priestly ministrations. Practice shifted to viewing the sacraments rather than participating in them, and elaborate stagings and visual dramatizations took over. Comforted by stories of the miraculous and by a proliferation of relics and popular devotions, the laity often preferred the security which these promised to the "distant" celebrations of sacramental grace. Miracle stories supplanted the persuasive power of participative symbols. A popular naive realism replaced the demanding ambiguity of faith.

The issue of sacramental causality dominated much of theological inquiry from the Middle Ages through the Counter-Reformation. "What causes sacraments to work?" Theologians never achieved a completely satisfactory intellectual explanation. Nor did the official teachers ever define the precise nature of this causality. The most adequate explanation relied on analogy. Sacraments work "in some way . . . like an instrument." The best theologians qualified their assertions so that they always maintained the mystery element. Today, theologians approach sacramental causality more through the "who" question than through the "how" question. *God* causes sacramental efficacy. Word and action "work" not simply because they are spoken and done, but because God acts in them and people respond to God's initiating power. Sacramental causality is an example of the biblical notion of covenant.

Even with God's action as their causal foundation, sacraments include certain ecclesial conditions for their validity, indeed their very existence. The church determines their legitimate matter (things, gestures, situation) and form (verbal formulae). The church insists that both the official minister and participants in sacramental action must intend to do what the church does in these ritual moments. The mad priest who says "this is my body" over all the bread in a Paris bakery does not here consecrate the Eucharist. Whatever the mouse that nibbles in a medieval tabernacle receives, it does not receive the body of the risen Lord.

Theological discussion of the sixteenth through the nineteenth centuries followed along the causality line. Controversies sharpened and focused on particular sacraments, especially baptism, the Eucharist, and orders. Reaction and over-reaction characterized the relationship between Reformers and Counter-Reformers. Questions regarding the number and efficacy of sacraments and the power of official ministers prevailed. Controversies blurred the difference between authentic theologies and popular superstitious practices. This was a time of abuses, defensiveness, digging in, and overstatement on all sides. Both Protestants and Catholics lost sight of the liturgical context without which sacraments make no sense nor do they exist at all.

The Reformers returned to Scripture for their theological base. There, they discovered that only baptism and the Lord's Supper were directly traceable to moments in the life of the historical Jesus. While the return to biblical sources was a healthy move, the Reformers stretched the baptismal and Eucharistic texts to read as the very words of Jesus. Some of the Reformers, notably Zwingli and those who followed his direction, continued the contrast mentality discussed above. "It's *only* a symbol." This bolstered the assertion that there was no objective efficacy (effect) to sacramental action, and that remembering did no more than to recall with reverence what Jesus had done in the past. Liturgical anamnesis had no present efficacy.

The Council of Trent and the intellectual tradition of the Jesuits largely localized the Counter-Reformation response. Drawing on the two sources of Scripture and (conciliar and papal) Tradition, the Counter-Reformers affirmed the sevenfold sacramental system. They too stretched the biblical texts to prove Jesus' institution of all seven. They also maintained the rich biblical notion of remembrance as bringing significant past moments effectively into the present. This enabled them to hold firmly to the objective, real presence of Christ in the sacraments, especially the action of the Eucharist. Unfortunately, late Scholasticism moved from this affirmation of objective efficacy to an objectivist, mechanistic view of sacramental presence. In their zeal to maintain the reality of this presence, they often offered explanations focused more on a physicalist Jesus than on the risen Christ. In their devotion to correct rubrical performance by the celebrant, they lost sight of the importance of an assembly gathered for prayer. The catechism of the Council of Trent, laudably intended as a partial response to questions, eclipsed other biblical, liturgical, and theological sources. It became the forerunner of the manual-style, "bottom-line," defensive approach which characterized many Roman Catholic theological texts until recent times.

Both among the Reformers and the Counter-Reformers, a trend toward polemic reductionism resulted in theological "shrinking." Minimalist expectations, separation of the sacramental sign from its liturgical context, and a fragmented approach to the various elements constituting that sign contributed to a loss of appreciation for the power of symbolic action. The recent liturgical renewal within respective Christian denominations and the ecumenical dialogue among them has introduced a welcome countertrend to this earlier situation.

D. OFFICIAL ROMAN CATHOLIC MAGISTERIAL TEACHING

The greater part of official Roman Catholic teaching on the sacraments occurs in the context of particular issues regarding particular sacraments, rather than in extensive doctrinal pronouncements on "sacraments in general." However, official teaching does affirm certain principles and positions clearly. Chapter XIII of the compilation, *The Christian Faith* presents major conciliar and papal statements on sacraments in general.[3] While the weight and definitiveness of the various statements differ according to the level of authority exercised and assent invoked, certain "constants" emerge clearly.

1. Context

Official statements on sacraments occur largely in documents issued between the thirteenth and twentieth centuries, with the sixteenth century Council of Trent issuing numerous canons on the sacraments. Scholars and officials of these times worked out of a pre-historical-critical awareness. Therefore, the data of biblical and historical research did not greatly inform their official statements. Today, theologians and authorities know the importance of literary genres, historical relativity, and theological intent in interpreting any dogmatic or doctrinal pronouncement.

A second contextual remark refers to the emotional tone of official teaching. Vatican II was not called to refute a particular set of problems, including a particular heresy. Pope John XXIII called it to advance the pastoral mission of the church. Therefore, its statements are characterized by a positive tone, a respect for richness and diversity, an

---

[3] J. Neuner and J. Dupuis, eds. *The Christian Faith* (New York: Alba House, 1982), pp. 365-381.

openness to the wide variety of perspectives which inform authentic catholic tradition. By contrast, most earlier sacramental statements were formulated out of a defensive situation, in response to threats real or perceived. They articulate one position over against another. They set negative limits on orthodox belief, carefully asserting what *not* to believe. Seldom if ever do they offer an extended treatment of what *to* believe. Statements on sacraments in general do not offer a full-blown theology. There is no strict, official dogmatic definition of sacrament. Rather, both in its positive descriptions and in its negative cautions, the magisterium carefully qualifies and delimits its teaching. "If anyone says that (these) sacraments are instituted only for the sake of nourishing the faith, *anathema sit.*" "If anyone says ... that faith alone in the divine promise is sufficient to obtain grace, *anathema sit.*"[4] Clearly, sacraments are meant to nourish the faith of those who participate in them. And clearly, faith in God's promise is an important component of the divine-human relationship. But the adverbial qualifiers *only* and *alone* establish negative limits to an orthodox attitude of belief.

2. Themes

a. The morals of the minister

From early times, the relationship between a minister's personal morals and the objective efficacy of a sacramental act has been a problem.[5] One can only imagine the pastoral desperation which would have evoked such concern, such insistence on clarification. In its affirmation of God's presence and power to effect sacramental grace, the church has maintained a position that guarantees God's availability to its members, no matter the personal worthiness or unworthiness of their ministers. While it would be naive to think that an official's life does not have an effect on the religious

---

[4]Ibid., p. 372, Items 1315 and 1318.

[5]Ibid., pp. 367-368, 372, Items 1301, 1303, 1304, and 1322.

health of his people, it is nevertheless true that the sacramental event does not *depend* on his virtue. Sacraments depend, causally, on the promise of God. The minister and participants do have to intend to do what the church does, because sacraments are the church's acts. But the church receives these acts because God loves people, not because anyone is worthy, either to preside over or to participate in them. This insistence on God's causality in the matter of grace is a variation on a theme deep within our Judeo-Christian tradition. It receives eloquent expression in an "election" text from the Book of Deuteronomy. "It was not because you were more in number than any other people that the Lord set his love upon you and chose you, for you were the fewest of all peoples; but it is because the Lord loves you" (Deuteronomy 6:7-8). God's love triumphs both over minority status and ministerial inadequacies.

b. Matter, form, and ecclesial decision

Ecclesial conditions for sacramental validity include the approved matter and form. In its official statements on this issue, the church often explicitly affirms its own power to determine and, indeed, to change that matter and form. In approving the reception of communion under one species, Trent declares "...that in the dispensation of the sacraments, provided their substance is preserved, the church has always had the power to determine or change, according to circumstances, times and places, what she judges more expedient for the benefit of those receiving them or for the veneration of the sacraments."[6] In his 1947 constitution on the sacrament of orders, Pius XII even more directly invoked the church's power to alter the matter and form of its sacramental rituals. "If the (same) handing over of the instruments has at some time been necessary, even for validity, in virtue of the will and precept of the Church, all know that the Church has the power to change and abrogate what

---

[6]Ibid., p. 373, Item 1324.

she has determined."[7] Such statements reveal the church's ownership of these actions and its clear sense of decision-making power regarding their matter and form.

c. Sacramental character

Numerous official statements make reference to the indelible sacramental character associated with baptism, confirmation, and orders. These statements do not elaborate on the precise nature of the sign. Rather, even these formal assertions leave some imprecision. They speak of ". . . a certain indelible sign distinguishing (the recipient) from others," a "kind of indelible spiritual sign by reason of which (these) sacraments cannot be repeated."[8] Such language leaves room for theological speculation regarding the sacramental character of these three sacraments. Today, the question is raised particularly with reference to the sacraments of confirmation and orders. If confirmation is theologically one with baptism, what more does it "confer," even in terms of relationship, on those who receive it? And if orders has to do with pastoral ministry and not simply with sacramental powers, what does its character mean when ministry is more and more engaged in by the non-ordained? In all three sacraments, what does it mean, concretely, to speak of an "indelible spiritual" sign?

d. Recent directions

Only within the past fifty years or so do official magisterial statements move out of a defensive posture and into a more positive mode with regard to sacraments. In his encyclicals *Mystici Corporis* (1943) and *Mediator Dei* (1947), Pius XII presents the sacraments as actions of Christ through the church. This maintains Christ's role in sacramental causality, but acknowledges the possibility (probability) of his "mediate" institution of most of the seven sacraments. Such an institution was accomplished in and through the faith-community as it structured its life down through the centu-

[7]Ibid., p. 506, Item 1737.

[8]Ibid., pp. 369-370, 372, Items 1308 and 1319.

ries. Pius also takes an important step in broadening the understanding of Christ's presence in the sacraments. From medieval times, discussion of the "real presence" had focused on transubstantiation of the Eucharistic elements of bread and wine. This is a true, but excessively narrow understanding. The Pope broadens the notion of presence to include "the whole conduct of the liturgy." Dimensions of Christ's presence include the sacrifice of the altar, the person of the minister, the eucharistic species, the (other) sacraments, prayer and praise offered to God.[9] Vatican II's *Sacrosanctum Concilium* echoes this broadened notion. In a phrase of enormous ecumenical significance, this document adds that Christ "is present in His word, since it is He himself who speaks when the Holy Scriptures are read in the Church."[10]

Within the past several years some official magisterial statements have returned to the cautionary tone of the Counter-Reformation. This is particularly true with regard to the sacraments of orders, the Eucharist, and the sacrament of reconciliation.[11] While theological caution and pastoral prudence are necessary and admirable, it would be regrettable if the broad, rich perspective that issued forth from Vatican II were to be replaced by a one-sided, overly defensive, fearful approach to the sacraments by their official conservators.

While official statements are important for setting "bottom line" beliefs, they may lead to a deficient understanding if they are taken out of context or if they are presumed to provide a full picture of sacramental thought. In the light of current knowledge, two areas need a nuanced interpretation. Earlier magisterial cautions maintain the dichotomous view between symbol and reality discussed above. Thus, they tend to downplay the human foundations of worship and the intimate relationship between the liturgical sign and the mys-

[9]Ibid., p. 377, Item 1331.

[10]Ibid., pp. 379-380, Item 1334.

[11]See, for example, Vatican Congregation to Bishops, "The Minister of the Eucharist." *Origins* 13 (Sept. 15, 1983), pp. 229-233 and Pope John Paul II, "The Meaning of Priesthood." *Origins* 13 (Sept. 22, 1983), pp. 257-260.

tery of which it is an expression. It is to be hoped that a more integrated view of symbol and reality will once again prevail, as it did in the rich Augustinian notion of sacramental signs. Second, while Trent rightly sought to avoid the subjectivism associated with "faith alone," subsequent teaching gave insufficient attention to the personal commitment required of sacramental participants. Only recently have Roman Catholic theologians dared to reassert the truth that, while faith alone is insufficient for sacramental efficacy, faith is necessary for any religious act which is more than a rote, mechanistic performance.

* * * * *

The ecclesiological foundations of sacraments illustrate the Roman Catholic understanding of the sacramental principle in the church. The changes throughout history show that, from its beginning, the church has known and exercised its own decisive power over the precise conditions of its sacramental life. While the substance of baptism has always been a water-bath and the substance of the Eucharist has always been the sharing of bread and wine, the precise mode of these rites, as of others, has changed according to theological insight and pastoral need. Sacraments are acts of Christ in and through the mediating activity of the church. The sacramental principle affirms the adequacy of the church's activity, whatever that may be, to place the whole of life under the influence of Christ. The ongoing decisions of this living community express the vivifying presence of the Holy Spirit. Its gradual, official acceptance of certain liturgical events as particular, privileged moments acts out its confidence that, in change as well as in stability, the Spirit continues to animate its life.

E. SACRAMENTAL DIALOGUE: VALIDITY AND FRUITFULNESS

It is clear that, while they seem to be rather simple words and gestures, sacraments partake of the complexity that marks all important realities. They are public, corporate, and personal actions. Though they are actions of the church in and through its members and ministers, they are also actions of God in Christ. The issues that have marked Christian sacramental life have been many and varied. One way to put them in an intelligible framework is to return to the covenant structure of God's initiative and human response. All sacramental questions are a variation on this theme. *Covenant* provides the theological context for examining the dialogue between sacramental validity and sacramental fruitfulness. An outline highlights the major historical and ecclesial aspects of this dialogue.

Dialogue

God's Action ←——————————→ *Human Response*

Validity: the effectiveness and availability of grace	*Fruitfulness:* the authenticity and appropriation of grace
Minimum question: What is sufficient for a valid sacrament? Matter, form, minister, intention. Official church sets minimum conditions.	*Maximum question:* What is the best attitude and preparation for sacramental participation? A human act is "more or less" adequate, complete, etc. Participants set personal conditions.
Emphasis: What God does in and through the community.	*Emphasis:* What human beings do with God's initiative.
technical formula: *ex opere operato* Efficacy of sacrament does not depend on minister's holiness, morals. Nor does participant's faith place any obligation on God's grace, since grace is gift.	*technical formula:* *ex opere operantis* Interior religious intent is necessary. Minimum disposition is to place no obstacle to grace: *non ponentibus obicem* (passive disposition). Maximum disposition is active prayer, adoration, faith, etc.

Note: later usage tended to forget original context and intent. Assumed that by acts of ministers and participants and by rite alone, grace was automatically due. Moved into mechanistic view that sacraments produce grace simply by their very correct performance. "Holy things."

Note: revised rituals recover personalist view of importance of co-operation with God's grace. Necessity that sacraments be a human act, that is, personal acceptance of God's grace. conferred by the church in and through the rite.

Intent of formula:
to insist that all grace is gift, from God's initiative. Because they are from God, sacraments are acts of God in Christ— therefore, in his power. In them, humans have an absolute pledge of God's saving presence and power, the possiblity of genuine transformation. God does what God promises.

Intent of formula:
to foster active appropriation, the free and responsible acceptance of God's grace. Authenticity means that, insofar as possible, interior dispositions and exterior acts match one another. Visible activity, including ritual, should match invisible intentions. Necessity of faith on part of community and individuals.

Cause of efficacy:
God's unconditional offer of salvation in Christ. The power, work of God in Christ.

Condition for efficacy:
human freedom, co-operating with and receiving worthily the grace of God in Christ.

Interest: sign is narrowed to what is necessary for validity. Defined matter (things, situation, gestures), form (words), minister, intention.

Interest: sign viewed from a broader perspective. What does the full sign, including active communal participation, teach about the effects of a sacrament? All ritual words and gestures (prayers, hymns, postures, etc.).

Contemporary Christians know the negative effects of an overemphasis on questions of validity. Reductionism results. The rich complexity of the dialogue between God and humankind is reduced to a magical, rote fulfilment of exterior observances. From the perspective of their historical context, both the Protestant Reformers and Catholic Counter-Reformers were defining minimum beliefs and describing "bottom line" practices. Both were preoccupied with clear, canonical regulations. In its decrees and canons, neither group purported to offer a full presentation of Christian sacramental life. Both inherited the unfortunate medieval development of sacraments understood apart from worship. When these actions began to be viewed in the abstract, apart from their liturgical context, their sign-value became minimized, if not lost. In their worship context, these symbols acted to dispose people to personal acts of praise, faith, thanksgiving, hope, and love. When this context receded, numerous privatized devotions and claims of miraculous apparitions filled the vacuum. Some were healthy, some not. Because they were largely unofficial in origin and sponsorship, they ran the risk of an unchecked enthusiasm.

Accompanying the loss of their worship context was a loss of the ecclesiological context of sacraments. Individuals asked, "What graces do *I* get? How are sacraments salvific for *me?*" People ran from Mass to Mass, accumulating for themselves graces from the infinite sacrifice of Calvary. Ordination conferred a personal power to confect the Eucharist and forgive sins. It was often seen more as a privilege than as a deputation to available service. Baptism snatched infants from Satan's clutches. Perhaps the most serious effect of this reductionism was the eclipse of the sacraments' whole pastoral context. Among many, overemphasis on validity led to the impression that all one had to do to receive sacraments worthily was to avoid mortal sin. Priests "dispensed," the laity "received" the sacraments. This fostered a passivity, a lessening of personal responsibility, a dichotomy between liturgical and pastoral activity. Such reductionism was detrimental, not only to sacramental, but to all dimensions of Christian life.

In our critical appraisal of earlier practice and our enthusiastic embrace of personal responsibility, we can neglect the other side of a fair critique. An overemphasis on fruitfulness runs the equal danger of reductionism. While our historical context calls us to embrace certain values and emphases of our time, we can run the risk of simply accommodating to our culture. We can forget that sacramental signs are also countersigns. They must both express and transform who we are and what our world is. A heightened emphasis on personal participation can place unrealistic expectations on the liturgy. It can ask that every sacramental event correspond perfectly to one's personal feelings at a given time, that every celebration provide an emotional "high." This is a new face to the old problem of pure subjectivity. It too is a loss of ecclesiological context, of the awareness that church and world are greater than any individual's experience of them. This attitude can foster a new individualism, a new unworthiness on the part of sacramental participants. No person can live, always, at a level of religious intensity. No single sacramental event can perfectly match every person's religious needs. No less than in the past, today's Christians must give themselves over to and participate in the God, the tradition, the message that exceed their individual needs, feelings, and desires.

One concrete example of the tendency toward this kind of reductionism arises among those for whom only aware, committed, consenting adults are "fit" subjects for Christian initiation. While the RCIA has provided a needed corrective to what Karl Rahner has termed "passive baptisms," the Roman Catholic church has maintained its practice of infant baptism as well. Literally, it avoids throwing out the baby with the bath. If we place too much weight on one's personal responsibility in the sacraments, we risk forgetting the most basic truth of our faith: God loves us first. God saves us. In a "healthy" infant baptism, the child becomes a powerful countersign to our culture's measurement of worth by productivity. He or she is a powerful sign that we humans do not create our salvation. We participate in it. In the dialogue between God and humankind, we receive God's grace which is larger than our individual concerns, accomplishments, and failures. We witness the fact that human dignity exceeds human productivity, that God's presence does not depend upon our personal worthiness.

The revised rites of Vatican II maintain the delicate balance between God's promise (emphasized by sacramental validity) and human response (emphasized by sacramental fruitfulness). They affirm the weight of individual and communal responsibility to live a committed life. Likewise, they affirm the weight of God's action in and through the church's symbolic signs. Sometimes, official words and gestures can weight individuals down. Ritual can be an oppressive burden. But sometimes, ritual's sustaining power can buoy up individuals, can carry them along. This is especially evident in the sacraments associated with limit-situations like illness and commitment. Especially in the events of anointing, marriage, and orders, the formal ritual functions to carry along the individuals involved. They are participating in a reality greater than they are: the mystery of human suffering and the mystery of human freedom. In such moments, emotions run high. In its ritual, the church provides words and gestures to express what people often cannot express on their own. Through its liturgy, the church frees them to enter into what God is doing with them at this moment in their lives.

The word *valid* comes from a Latin adjective meaning *strong, powerful, efficacious.* If sacraments are really valid, then they must have power. This is not only the power of an authorized minister. Rather, sacramental celebrations must also make space for the power of symbolic activity to disclose their truth and thus to become really efficacious among people. They must enable the mystery of God's presence to shine forth and thus to illuminate our individual and communal lives. Over the course of time, they must empower people to work toward transformation, the transformation of their personal lives and of the societies in which they live. Otherwise, these sacraments may be canonically correct, but they are hardly *valid* in the sense that they make a difference for good within and among people.

III. Supportive Readings

Many readings from the previous chapters on historical context and Christology are also useful for an ecclesiological understanding. In addition, the following are helpful.

— Kilmartin, Edward. "A Modern Approach to the Word of God and Sacraments of Christ." In Francis Eigo, ed. *The Sacraments: God's Love and Mercy Actualized.* Philadelphia: Villanova University Press, 1979, pp. 59-109.

> This article is very good on the history and concepts of classical sacramental theology. It uses and explains technical terminology well. It is sensitive to the contributions and challenges of Protestant theologians, especially Karl Barth and Emil Brunner. It is difficult, but worth the reading.

— Rahner, Karl. *The Church and the Sacraments.* New York: Herder and Herder, 1968.

> This classic text presents the church as the fundamental sacrament, and the various individual sacraments as acts in which the church's sacramental nature is fulfilled. It is a clear, contemporary presentation of grace, causality, the institution of the sacraments, and sacramental piety.

— Vaillancourt, Raymond. *Toward a Renewal of Sacramental Theology.* Collegeville: The Liturgical Press, 1979, pp. 41-47.

> This short section on "Ecclesiology and the Sacraments" presents the history behind ecclesiological renewal and the effects of that renewal on sacramental thought and practice.

6

Eschatological Foundations of Sacramental Action

I. Orienting Questions and Readings

A. What is your understanding of "eschatology"?

On a human level, what makes you feel "one" with another person or other persons? What makes you "one" on the level of faith?

In what sense do you understand the claim, "Sacraments are efficacious signs"?

B. Read the World Council of Churches' document *Baptism, Eucharist and Ministry* (Faith and Order paper Number 111) with an eye toward its eschatological foundations and implications.

II. Reflections

A. THE MEANING OF ESCHATOLOGY

In classical Scholastic theology, eschatology was a study of the four last things: death, judgment, heaven, and hell. Informed by a more biblical and wholistic perspective, contemporary theologians view eschatology as a dimension of every aspect of Christian life and thought. Therefore, in a sense, the eschatological foundations of sacraments are implicit in all the preceding chapters. But in another sense, eschatology does bear studying in its own right. It is a prospective view of human existence "...from (man's) present situation in saving history, governed by the event of Jesus Christ, to the final fulfilment of his own existential situation, which is already eschatologically determined." Eschatology "applies to the present insofar as the last days have begun in Christ ('God's eschatological action'); where it seems to refer to the future alone, it means the future as interpreting the present."[1] It is the study of the coming of the reign of God, and of all areas of our tradition from the perspective of the "already but not yet" character of that coming. Eschatology explores the signs of promise and hope between Christ's first and final coming. It is action-oriented, insisting that the reign of God begun in Jesus Christ is both a gift which humankind must receive in thanksgiving and a task which it must embrace in responsibility. Eschatology is grounded in God, the ultimate mystery, the presence that both reveals and conceals itself in and through the ambiguous signs of our history. It springs from the conviction that God's self-giving continues to manifest itself long after the days of Jesus' historical visibility on earth.

Like the reign of God and like all things human, sacraments too are "already, but not yet" realities. Each has a past, present, and future structure. The familiar hymn of Thomas Aquinas expresses this threefold dynamic well. "O Sacred Banquet, in which Christ is received, the memory of his passion recalled, and a pledge of future glory given." Each sacrament recalls a definitive past event, the death-resurrection of Jesus Christ. Each expresses a particular present grace rooted in that past event - a grace of healing, welcome, nourishment, commitment. The eschatological, future-oriented dimension holds prominence when the church is exposed to persecution and martyrdom. And, though this

---

[1]"Eschatology," In Karl Rahner and Herbert Vorgrimler, *Theological Dictionary* (New York: Crossroad, 1981), pp. 150 and 152.

dimension has lain dormant in the shadows of theological speculation for a long time, it is re-emerging out of the pressured areas in which the church is fighting to be church today. Thus, each sacrament looks toward a future in hope that the victorious death-resurrection of the Lord will, in fact, make a definitive difference and come to perfect fulfilment.

Like the Gospel itself, each sacrament is a sign of the reign of God, proclaiming its genuine and effective presence in space and time. Building on the role of the Holy Spirit in ongoing history, each sacrament appears more as a dynamic process than a static object, more a verb than a noun, more future-oriented than confined either to past or present. Each sacrament is both a sign and a countersign. Therefore, each both resists identifying this world and God's reign, and resists positing a complete dichotomy between them. Affirmation and critique of all things human maintains a delicate and necessary balance.

While the eschatological dimension of many sacramental themes is re-emerging, two current directions of thought deserve special attention. They build greatly on the unfinished, partial, and provisional character of all reality viewed from this future-oriented perspective. In ecumenical dialogue, theologians and officials are exploring the "already but not yet" fact of greater convergence yet fragmented agreement. They seek a solid theological basis which would justify moving together in the ongoing quest "that all may be one." And liberation theologies of all kinds adopt an eschatological perspective in their insistence that making a difference for good, here and now in human history, does contribute to the building and definitive coming of God's reign. These two directions form the structure of this chapter. As we shall see below, they cannot be completely separated from one another, because coming together in unity and working together for God's reign are two sides of the same coin, the "cash-value" of our Christian belief. But for purposes of logic we may examine each in its own right and for its particular eschatological foundation.

B. ECUMENICAL DIALOGUE: THE QUEST FOR AN ELUSIVE UNITY

1. The Current Situation

In the wake of Vatican II, Christians of many denominations began to engage in ecumenical dialogue with evangelistic fervor. Theological commissions, parish study groups, interfaith worship services, television programs: all signaled a serious attack on the long-standing animosity and mutual ignorance among divided members of the same body. On a very concrete level, common struggles like U.S. civil rights efforts, neighborhood revitalization, and the amelioration of poverty put people of similar religious convictions though dissimilar religious confessions side by side on picket-lines, sit-ins, and at voter registration booths.

Recently, the thrust toward ecumenical agreement seems to have stalled in many quarters at the official level. Still, many ordinary Christians who have come to know one another as brothers and sisters in a faith-commitment across denominational lines continue, formally and informally, to explore their commonalities. They seek a way to let a prior though hidden unity arise and overcome well-established and, in some cases, well-entrenched historical divisions. And the 1982 Lima document on baptism, eucharist, and ministry is a tangible theological expression of areas of convergence among major Christian groups. This document is not merely an intellectual exercise. The text, and the efforts that preceded and proceed from it, arise from "the holy restlessness that comes out of the urge to worship the one and true God with groans too deep for words, and which will not settle for anything short of what Christ promised."[2]

2. Theological Anchors

What theological themes ground this well-intentioned quest for unity? What breadth of vision informs this search?

[2]Franz J. van Beeck, *Grounded in Love: Sacramental Theology in an Ecumenical Perspective* (Washington, D.C.: University Press of America, 1981), p. 4.

Clearly, it is the articulation of the common ground behind our denominational differences. Such a foundation goes back beyond the political and theological disputes of the sixteenth century, to a common humanity and a common theological tradition which have both a logical and an historical priority over the Reformation and Post-Reformation debates. In his book *Grounded in Love,* Franz van Beeck proposes several fundamental themes which direct and inform current ecumenical probing. All contain the eschatological dimension of provisionality and future-orientation noted above. I shall borrow and expand on his categories, in setting forth the key awarenesses affecting ecumenical theology today.

a. Anthropology, Theology, and Christology

As suggested in Chapter Two, our common humanity grounds all further commonalities of faith, doctrine, or practice. Celebrating shared human life is the basis for all sacramental action. From their eschatological perspective, sacraments celebrate the human attitude of hope. Hope is the human response to God's saving activity in human history, an activity already yet not fully experienced. According to Geoffrey Wainwright, sacraments are "non-exclusive promises" of God to which humans look as a sign (foretaste, pledge, downpayment) of future realization. In a very true sense, we humans do not hope for what is totally unknown and alien to us. We hope for what, even dimly, we already know. And so, we come to the Eucharistic table not yet to become sated on the reign of God but to taste it. We approach this meal "to try the relish," to experience "both the provisionality and yet the genuineness of the kingdom as it flavours the present."[3] Similarly, the other sacraments offer a hint of what awaits us when God shall truly be all in all. Marriage is a sign of covenant fidelity, baptism and confirmation of God's loving welcome and our committed

---

[3]Geoffrey Wainwright, *Eucharist and Eschatology* (New York: Oxford University Press, 1981), p. 152.

response. Anointing promises a healing here that must suffice "until every tear shall be wiped away." Reconciliation with our brothers and sisters is a shadow of the final, joyful "coming home" that awaits us. Orders mirrors the triumph over chaos that characterizes life in the reign of God.

The other side of the sacramental dialogue is the theological, what God does. Again, eschatology enters in. We believe that God's self-giving continues to be present and seek expression in human history, long after Jesus' historical visibility on earth. In this time between Jesus' first and final coming, God uses the same means of self-giving as we humans do. God uses signs. These signs, including our official sacraments, are not merely manifestations of a common past. As important if not more so, they are pledges of a common future. Of all the sacraments, the Eucharist has probably received the most "eschatological" attention. Liturgists point out the past-present-future structure of each eucharistic prayer. Theologians have rediscovered the biblical and patristic image of heavenly banquet as having equal weight with the more medieval images of unbloody sacrifice, representation of Calvary, etc. In this vein, Max Thurian picks up the thread that runs through many current writings. "The Church today needs to recall (this) cosmic, ecological, positive and optimistic view of the eucharist, and to celebrate it in a liturgy which expresses heavenly joy on earth and expectation of the banquet in the kingdom of God."[4] This shared meal becomes the pre-eminent symbol of God's will and, indeed, of God's hope for the human race: that, some day, all people will live in covenant, partnership, equality, solidarity, and mutual nourishing. Viewed from the perspective of heavenly banquet, the eucharist is the sign of what the Christian household and humankind ought to be.

In and through the created signs of the sacraments, believers "wait in hope for the manifestation of God's new creation

---

[4]Max Thurian, "The Eucharistic Memorial, Sacrifice of Praise and Supplication." In Max Thurian, ed., *Ecumenical Perspectives on Baptism, Eucharist and Ministry* (Geneva: World Council of Churches, 1983), p. 97.

and for the time when God will be all in all."[5] This statement links eschatology with an earlier theme, that of the sacramental principle. This principle posits the capacity of relative, finite, material realities to mediate God's loving presence. It endows ordinary life with the possibility, the holiness of God's creative power. In people and things, words and gestures, God throws forward some part of the future into the present as promise. Material creation is destined to be both the scene and the vehicle of the communion which God intends, now and in the future, with humankind. Wainwright's commentary on key New Testament eschatological texts makes this point well:

> ...in becoming the vehicle of saving fellowship between God and man, the bread and wine of the eucharist are granted, at least in a hidden way, fulfilment of the destiny after which the whole material creation groans (cf. Rom. 8:19–23)...The eschatological condition in which God will be all in all (I Cor 15:28) is envisaged by the New Testament as new heavens and a new earth (II Pet 3:13), peopled by men and women in their risen and glorified *bodies* (I Cor 15:35–58; Phil 3:21).[6]

Thus, God and humankind, matter and spirit, present action and future promise are united here and now, in reality and in hope.

In our Christian tradition, the theological foundation of our faith does not rest in a God who remains a distant, unfathomable mystery. Our God has come irrevocably among us in the person and message of Jesus Christ, preacher of God's eschatological reign. A great deal of Christological inquiry into the sacraments has focused on Jesus' presence, especially in the Eucharist. Controversy has

[5] *Baptism, Eucharist and Ministry.* Text in the *International Review of Mission,* Vol. LXXII (April 1983). Text on "Baptism III, Article 9." Subsequent references appear as *BEM* in the body of the chapter.

[6] Wainwright, *op. cit.,* p. 149.

swirled around the nature and reality of his presence, and its link (or non-link) to Jesus' self-gift in the past historical event of his death. Until recently, the question of Jesus' sacramental presence has not exploited what was undoubtedly a biblical theme, namely the future and definitive presence of the risen Lord. Slowly but surely, a shift is occurring in this direction. Much of current New Testament scholarship now emphasizes the anticipatory, eschatological character of these first Christian writings, the fact that the earliest communities lived in lively expectation of their Lord's imminent return. While that return did not happen precisely as they had expected, the thread of Jesus' coming continues throughout Christian life and thought. Donald Gray picks up this theme, suggesting that one of the ways out of the controversial impasse of "real presence" discussions is to approach Jesus' eucharistic presence in terms of the mode of futurity. He writes:

> The liturgical prayer *Maranatha,* which is most probably to be translated "Come, Lord," suggests not simply a petition requesting the immediate coming into the midst of the eucharistic assembly on the part of the risen Jesus, but also and what is more important, points ahead in time to the definitive coming into the midst which is termed the parousia, or presence.[7]

The model of futurity picks up a theme discussed in Chapter Three, that is, the simultaneity of God's presence and absence, revealing and concealing, reality and non-exhaustive expression in any and all sacramental signs. Like the unfathomable mystery of God whenever that mystery comes to expression in space and time, the mode of futurity acknowledges the risen Lord's real presence, but a presence neither exhaustive nor definitive "until he comes in glory." "The anamnesis in which Christ acts through the joyful celebration of His Church is thus both representation and anticipation. It is not only a calling to mind of what is past and its

[7]Donald Gray, "The Real Absence: A Note on the Eucharist." *Worship* 44 (1970), p. 23.

significance. It is the Church's effective proclamation of God's mighty acts and promises." (*BEM*, Eucharist II, Art. 7). As part of the interim situation of church and world between Jesus Christ's resurrection and the *eschaton,* sacraments are provisional, anticipatory signs of his future non-provisional, definitive coming.

Another Christological interest appears in the writings of some theologians concerned with the relationship between eschatology and sacraments. In addition to examining the Gospel texts for their future-directedness, they also examine Jesus' actions with an eye toward their ecumenical implications. The feeding miracles are interpreted as signs of divine largesse. "Jesus apparently provided food for as many as came to hear him, without inquiring into their credentials."[8] In this vein, Jesus' propensity for eating with sinners gives a clear signal that the Eucharist is not primarily for the perfect, not a reward for virtue. Rather, this meal with and of Jesus is a means of evangelizing. It is a way of drawing people, especially those who most need God's nourishing love, into the Lord's transforming presence, his power to move from death to life. In this regard, Wainwright's exegesis of Luke 14:23 is most enlightening. Seen in its context of the parable of the great eschatological supper, "Compel them to come in" becomes a negative critique of current polities which require people to demonstrate Christian knowledge and virtues before they are invited to partake of God's sustaining meal.

b. Worship

The renewed awareness of worship as a primary theological source has focused renewed attention on the nature of this corporate ritual activity. Its eschatological dimension quickly becomes apparent. A reading of any official liturgical texts, past or present, gives evidence of the future-orientation of each sacramental event. The Lima liturgy prays to God to "...guide us towards the perfect unity of

---

[8] Wainwright, *op. cit.,* p. 129.

your Kingdom for ever." It links present experience with the hope of future fulfilment. "Now that we have tasted of the banquet you have prepared for us in the world to come, may we all one day share together the inheritance of the saints in the life of your heavenly city."

A more extended consideration of the eschatological dimension of the church follows below. But here it is appropriate to emphasize the community-shaping character of worship, especially common worship among Christians of various denominations. Both eschatology and behavior studies contribute to the thorny issue of intercommunion. If our behavior shapes our understanding, then would not common behavior (worship) shape a common theological understanding? Most theological objections to eucharistic intercommunion center around the fact that the Eucharist is a sign of unity. And if that unity is not perfectly realized, if theological consensus is not yet formulated, then is it not illegitimate to come together around a common table? Many see in the eschatological dimension of the sacraments a way to celebrate authentically together. They acknowledge that unity among Christians is not perfectly achieved. At this stage in history, it would be naive to claim otherwise. But we do hope together for a common unity. We do strive together for it. Might we not "anticipate" it in eucharistic communion? Perhaps, joint worship and joint sacramental celebrations could help to shape the unity we long for. Perhaps, unity in creed and order are not the ultimate norms for intercommunion. More fundamental, perhaps, is our unity in hope. Perhaps it is important to stress the causative, creative value of common worship as causative and creative of the oneness which God, Christ, and the now-fragmented Body hope for. Perhaps, common worship is more important for what it makes of us than for what it expresses as already true of us. Perhaps, intercommunion should be viewed more as a duty than as an interdiction.

c. Witness

"Actions speak louder than words." This familiar proverb implies the importance of Christian witness in any consideration of eschatology and the sacraments. Later reflections on liberation theologies will underscore this theme more in detail. Here, it suffices to draw attention to the link between Christian sacraments and their Old Testament roots, prophetic acts. Sacraments are Christian instances of what the ancient Hebrews called ôt, an act with a message. Sacraments and lives must proclaim a congruent message. Sacraments must teach their participants less the correct niceties of orthodox doctrine than the deep demands of Christian life. Believers live in hope of the reign of God. Their every action, including every sacramental action, contributes to shaping God's reign, making it present, provisional and partial as that presence may now be. Lives are sacramental insofar as in and through them God's self-giving love radiates and "God is alive and well in the world." Thus, the Christian not only believes in the future, but lives from it. This means that the eschatological future of God's glorious reign (already begun and announced in and through Jesus' resurrection) grounds his or her piety and politics, attitudes and actions. These ethical implications begin at the beginning, with baptismal initiation.

> As they grow in the Christian life of faith, baptized believers demonstrate that humanity can be regenerated and liberated. They have a common responsibility, here and now, to bear witness together to the Gospel of Christ, the Liberator of all human beings. (*BEM,* Baptism III, Article 10).

This same principle holds true for the Eucharist. "As participants in the eucharist,...we prove inconsistent if we are not actively participating in (this) ongoing restoration of the world's situation and the human condition." (*BEM,* Eucharist II, Article 20).

In true biblical fashion, witness is the fruit by which the world knows sacramental efficacy. When the witness of holy lives cuts across canonical lines, that is a unity more basic than any denominational divisions, more harmonious than any creedal discord. It may even be easier to envision a future unity of official formulation than a unity of lives giving eloquent testimony to the Gospel of Jesus Christ. But, in the spirit of eschatological hope, this too is a oneness both to be striven for and celebrated (brought to expression and causatively shaping) in the daily actions of Christian lives.

d. The Holy Spirit

Classical Western theology has been stronger in its development of thought regarding law and sin than it has been in its theology of the Holy Spirit. Nevertheless, pneumatology increasingly occupies the attention of Western thinkers today. Perhaps this is due to an increasing influence of Eastern categories on Western thought. Perhaps it stems from a renewed interest in the God of mystery, the breath who "blows where he will." Perhaps one might attribute it to an active and dynamic view of creation, to historical studies on the important role of the epiklesis in each sacramental event, or to the growing experience of the "unknown" in human life. Certainly, *BEM* breathes the air of Spirit-theology, a theology irrevocably bound to the document's future orientation. A few texts illustrate this point well.

> God bestows upon all baptized persons the anointing and the promise of the Holy Spirit, marks them with a seal and implants in their hearts the first instalment of their inheritance as sons and daughters of God. The Holy Spirit nurtures the life of faith in their hearts until the final deliverance when they will enter into its full possession, to the praise of the glory of God. (*BEM,* Baptism II, Article 5).

> . . . the Church prays to the Father for the gift of the Holy Spirit in order that the eucharistic event may be a reality: the real presence of the crucified and risen Christ giving his life for all humanity. (*BEM,* Eucharist II, Article 14).

> The Holy Spirit through the Eucharist gives a foretaste of the Kingdom of God: the Church receives the life of the new creation and the assurance of the Lord's return (*BEM,* Eucharist II, Article 18).

In each of the above, the Lima text links the Spirit's sacramental activity with a final, eschatological hope. Many aspects of this pneumatological approach are congenial to persons with ecumenical interests. Perhaps the line of thought which offers the best possibilities for fruitful development is that which tries to see a way through the strictures of current legal structures. By definition and by biblical witness, the Spirit of God cannot be captured — in neat categories, among certain people, or in only specified situations. The Spirit both inspires and exceeds all formulations, all expectations. Van Beeck sees ecumenical hope in the "one Spirit that must be allowed to animate as well as blow apart the great variety of separated ministrations."[9] Reverence for the Spirit's power acknowledges that nothing so rich as sacraments can be brought entirely within the confines of legislative definition. While ecclesial order is eminently important, it is never the ultimate religious value. Like the Spirit, all questions of order, polity, and validity are at the service of God's creative, surprising action in the church and world. Like the Spirit, all structures are to free and not to numb, to convince and not to coerce, to empower and not to paralyze. Dogma, order, all human expressions of the divine mystery are essentially provisional. They may never try to "tie salvation down," never claim exclusive or absolute possession of God's saving truth. They must function in service of a dynamic faith, not as a substitute for it. In the shadow of the Spirit's wings, anything can happen!

3. *Ecclesiology: the Pilgrim People on Their Way*

On a practical level, ecumenical issues regarding the sacraments come to rest in the question of the nature of the church. If our primary ecclesial image is that of a perfect society, a self-sufficient institution in the manner of Robert Bellarmine's definition, then until all segments of that society are a perfect fit or until all aspects of the institution are

---

[9]van Beeck, *op, cit.,* p. 6.

perfectly aligned, communal worship, especially eucharistic worship, makes no sense. But if our primary image is more dynamic and eschatological, then new possibilities surface in our consciousness. Both in the New Testament and in Vatican II, the dominant ecclesial image is that of a pilgrim people on their way. Such an image recognizes that everything in historical existence is partial and provisional. Thus, any unity, including that of creed and order, is approximate. It is a shape always in the shaping, a unity *in via* more than *in statu*. Structures as well as limits are always somewhat indefinite and sliding, never perfectly congruent with the eschatological reign of God.

But the image also offers us another truth. In it, the church is not only an institution. It is also an event: people moving together in the same direction. This people is a verb as well as a noun, a process as well as a structure. Taken in conjunction with the insight that the church's sacramental actions both express and shape its identity, one might argue that it is imperative for the Christian churches to come together in worship *so that* unity in the one faith may grow among them.

4. Sacraments: A Model of Futurity

Because the classical images of heaven, hell, church, and sacraments have been primarily spatial, it is difficult for our imaginations to break out of these categories. Especially with regard to the Eucharist, the pre- and post-Reformation controversies over "real presence" solidified this localizing tendency. Such a tendency has a certain natural psychological appeal. If we can locate something, we feel secure. We can handle it, even if the "it" is a difficult problem. We can rule out a certain ambiguity. If my class notes are on my desk, they are not lost. I can use them. I can control this portion of my life.

And so it has been with a spatial concept of sacraments. In them, God is "there" and not necessarily elsewhere. In a sense, God's presence is able to be "called down" and, therefore, controlled. At its best, such imagery has offered great comfort and assurance to people when everything else in their lives was "up for grabs." At its worst, spatial imagery has fostered attitudes and behavior of manipulating magic.

Recently, some theologians have suggested that spatial categories are not the ones most appropriate for forming sacramental consciousness. Including Edward Schillebeeckx, many have moved more into interpersonal images. These seem a more adequate way of expressing the dynamic, mutual character of these covenant-events. A second set of categories has entered the picture. Whether or not they have explicitly formulated it as such, theologians focusing strongly on the eschatological dimensions of sacraments show a natural affinity for temporal imagery. These categories are less easily pinned down, but just as real, for us creatures who live out our existence not only in space but also in time. Such theologians easily adopt a model of futurity. They echo the Heideggerian insight that, in one sense, the past-present-and future dimensions of human reality are simultaneous. These dimensions interpenetrate one another. But the future has a certain priority, because that is where we are going.

For those buoyed up by the possibilities of a liberal theological tradition, this emphasis on the future is both congenial and exciting. It views sacraments not primarily as relics from our past, but as actions which do lead us into a new age. But even persons of a more sober bent may find this approach to the sacraments attractive. Today, we recognize as never before that the future may be menacing as well as meaningful, an occasion for horror as well as for hope. Donald Gray expresses this truth eloquently.

> In general the future reaches man in an ambiguous form — it may suggest hope and expectation on the one hand or meaninglessness and despair on the other. The future may nourish and build up or it may deprive and tear down. The Christian is not rescued from the ambiguity of the immediate future through the eucharist, but he is rescued from the terror of ultimate meaninglessness by the coming into the present of the ultimate future in the eucharist...through the provisional and anticipatory presence of the ultimate future the

> Christian is enabled to go out into every immediate future without terror. The eucharistic presence of the ultimate future sustains our presence in every immediate future.[10]

This is a bold affirmation of faith. It admits that we can never completely control our lives. It embraces the fundamental ambiguity of human existence. In this perspective, sacraments are not so much answers to our human problems. Rather, they are moments in which people live through and live with their questions together. Sacraments are less an insurance policy than a promissory note, less a package than a pledge. God is here, hidden but real. God never promises to remove human pain, only to walk with people through it. "I *will be* your God." Always.

C. THEOLOGIES OF LIBERATION

The Latin American version of Liberation Theology has received the lion's share of attention, including magisterial attention. But it is not the only system of thought which may be designated a theology of liberation. Indeed, any approach which takes the perspective of the "underside of history," any viewpoint which claims a kind of oppression as its source and a kind of freedom as its goal falls into this category. Black theology, feminist theology, theologies emanating from second or third world countries or from any group which lacks the power to determine its own destiny may justly be considered a theology in service of liberation. This chapter shall not espouse the particular perspective of any one of these. Rather, we shall isolate certain common themes which inform any liberationist approach, exploring their import for sacramental thought and practice.

1. An Eschatological Base

As noted earlier in this chapter, the dominant approach to eschatology today is neither individualistic nor other-

---

[10]Gray, *op. cit.*, p. 25.

worldly. Neither "my salvation" nor an over-spiritualized heaven unconnected with life here and now holds center stage. The goal of salvation, as of the Christian's cooperation in God's saving work, is corporate, cosmic, and historical. From a liberationist perspective, any eschatology which denies historical progress toward the establishment of God's definitive reign does not do justice to the intimate connection between this world and the next, much less to God's creative, powerful Spirit. A hope which does not issue in concrete action is no hope at all.

This approach in no way pretends to identify God's reign and this world, social progress and ultimate salvation. It adopts no utopian vision of perfect light, peace, and justice here and now. However, it does call on Christian religious imagination to see in our world and in all human relationships a symbolic realization of God's covenant with the entire human family. It posits a world in which God's creative, redeeming love acts not only *on* human life, but *in* and *through* it.

> The church cannot claim to be complete in itself at any time within the historical realm. Its perfection and fulness are to be attained by the power of the Holy Spirit in the *eschaton,* when the entire creation is redeemed and brought to subjection to the Father by the Son (I Cor 15:24-26). To be engaged in service towards the bringing about of this final goal in the power of the risen Lord is the mission of the Church.[11]

One must maintain the dialectical tension between church-world and God's final reign. But one must never totally dichotomize them.

This view of God's eschatological activity is a strong counterforce to a purely privatized, spiritual, passively receptive stance. It locates God's saving activity in this world, a world

---

[11]V.C. Samuel, "The Mission Implications of *Baptism, Eucharist and Ministry,"* *International Review of Mission* LXXII (April 1983), p. 207.

gradually being transformed into the next. This approach is an example of that sacramental principle which takes material reality seriously. Though neither the church nor secular society equals the reign of God, both are the arenas in which the reality of that reign breaks in or it doesn't, becomes actual or it doesn't in human lives. *Arena* is a deliberate term, because much of human life, especially for society's have-nots, is a struggle — to the death. God's reign breaks in in those borderline areas where church and world struggle for truth and justice. God's reign will come about in and through the overcoming of evil by good in human history, or not at all. This overcoming includes a liberation of body, mind, and spirit — not only for individuals, but for whole peoples. It works toward systems of politics, education, economics, and health-care which really free people to live a more human, humane existence.

2. The Church's Mission

A sacramental church *is* a church in mission, in service of a world and a God larger than itself. The mission is one of human liberation — from individual and societal sin, from personal and corporate evil. In no small measure, it includes an earthly liberation. Such a goal stems not merely from restlessness with the *status quo,* but from a conscious faith. Real faith in the God who transcends history knows that it has nothing to lose.

> The Christian revolution consists in setting in motion, within the community, signs which presuppose that insecurity has been overcome and which commit man to a new risk. It is the risk of bringing a message to the surrounding community. Like the message of the Master himself, it must be a critical message carried to a community where the transcendent has been put in the service of man's security.[12]

[12]Juan L. Segundo, *The Sacraments Today* (Maryknoll, New York: Orbis, 1974), p. 32.

Like the Baptist, the church becomes a voice crying in the world and acting out that cry. Like Jesus of Nazareth, the church is sent into the world to witness that God is near —by words and deeds, by spiritual and physical signs. Like Jesus, the church must prefer to expend its energies among the needy, the outcasts, those whom the dominant society considers less worthy of its attention, when it considers them at all. Otherwise, the church risks becoming an accomplice to the demonic powers at work in the world. Its God risks becoming merely the legitimizer of a stable, if unjust social order. Its sacraments become efficacious signs of a religion which is patronizing, pacifying, and palliative.

One of the sharpest critiques of the church's failure in this regard comes from an Asian theologian in remarks on the Eucharist. It is a global condemnation, framed in very traditional language.

> When the Eucharist ceases to relate to integral human liberation, it ceases to be connected with Christ's life sacrifice: it does not then build human community; it does not, therefore, help constitute the kingdom of God on earth: it does not even honor God objectively. . . The Eucharist is in captivity. It is dominated by persons who do not experience oppression in their own selves. The Eucharist will not be liberated to be true to its mission so long as the churches are captive within the world's power establishments. . . It is when Christians make a fundamental option against oppression, and struggle against it, that the Eucharist itself will be liberated.[13]

This critique is not simply based on a hope for our common human future. In the tradition of the Hebrew prophets, it excoriates those powers, religious or secular, which keep people down. It is rooted in a profound belief: that Christ's presence *is* real and effective in concrete history, that our

---

[13]Tissa Balasuriya, *The Eucharist and Human Liberation* (Maryknoll, New York: Orbis, 1979), pp. 38 and 62.

memorials of that presence do not leave the world un-
changed, but better for their having been celebrated. It issues
a challenge that such celebrations not be empty, not indiffer-
ent to the lives of those who do and do not participate in
them. At their best, Eucharists are a celebration of human
solidarity and mutual care. In them, God's purpose for
humankind is both glimpsed and realized in and through the
signs of bread broken and feeding, wine poured out and
passed around. Commenting on the three realities which
form the subject-matter of the document *Baptism, Eucharist
and Ministry,* William Lazareth puts it succinctly yet clearly:

> Baptism, eucharist and ministry were given by God not as
> doctrines to be debated by divided churches, but as healing
> and uniting signs of a church living and working for a
> renewed and unified humankind...The incredibility of the
> Christian message is often vitiated by the non-credibility of
> the Christian messengers.[14]

The church *goes to work* with what God gives it, including
what God gives it to do.

From a liberationist perspective, baptism has less to do
with gaining new members and more to do with getting
more members to commit themselves to working for the
betterment of humankind. To be plunged into the waters of
dying and rising is to be immersed in the very center of the
struggle for human freedom. Baptism enlists persons in the
service of the *one* Lord of the universe. No other gods need
apply. Reconciliation has less to do with feeling good that
the burden of my sins is lifted, and more to do with becoming reconciling agents amid the fragmented, vested interests
of an unreconciled society. Repentance is sorrow for one's
individual and communal complicity in the exploitation of
oppressed nations, classes, and an oppressed sex. Orders has
less to do with hierarchical status and more to do with official public leadership of a faith-community in service of a

---

[14]William Lazareth, "Guest Editorial." *International Review of Mission* LXXII
(April 1983), pp. 154-155.

more humane world. Proclaiming God's Word includes giving voice to the voiceless, whatever their religious affiliation. The Eucharist memorializes Jesus insofar as, in their own lives, its celebrants image his self-gift of solidarity and struggle with the poor. To make a remembrance of *this* man is to live under the sign of his cross, insofar as we too give ourselves over to death on behalf of others. It is to know that in and through death, not around it, comes resurrection.

> No broken bread can be a remembrance of the death of Jesus if it is divorced from the brokenness of the people, from the death of their children for lack of bread, and the suffering meted out to the masses with whom Jesus identifies.[15]

In our tradition, if the Eucharist is a symbol of unity, it is not the cozy unity of those who feel good about themselves and one another. It is the unity of those who struggle together toward the oneness of all humanity, a unity that we may even begin to know here on earth, when our society comes to look more and more like God's reign. World unity is world justice.

Because they reverence the things of the earth, the sacraments are a protest against materialistic exploitation. Because they are communal actions, they are a protest against alienation. In their celebration, what is called for is a conversion of heart and imagination: from self-perfection to the establishment of humane structures; from a patronizing mercy to a merciful justice; from the security of one's personal growth to the risk of societal rejection. That is the never-ending task of people who know that they are always "on the way."

The church's mission is not only to be a sign on earth of God's all-embracing love. It is also to be a countersign against the temptation to idolize any human movement, any

---

[15]Samuel Rayan, "The Lima Text and Mission." *International Review of Mission* LXXII (April 1983), p. 204.

single moment. In particular, a highly sacramental religion must walk the delicate balance between affirming the good things of this world and God's mediating activity through creation, and critiquing all things human in light of the partial, provisional character of our existence. Those who remember the "already but not yet," the eschatological foundations of our faith, will resist the temptation to worship false gods, even the false god of religion. They will remember that sacraments mediate but do not exhaust the reality of God. These actions draw us forward, through the darkness of human struggle, to the Light that beckons all people to come, at the end, and be "at home" in God.

3. Ecumenical Possibilities: Intercommunion

Not only does the overall umbrella of "eschatological foundations" offer possibilities for progress toward intercommunion among members of now-divided Christian churches. A liberationist perspective as well presents intercommunion both as a possibility and as a challenge. When they ask, "In what does Christian unity consist?" many sincere believers today hear a new voice in their hearts. The answer does not focus on canonical regularity, nor even on perfect creedal harmony. Today, many persons acknowledge that major divisions among Christians cut across denominational lines. Many hold *the* dividing line between real difference and commonality to be whether or not believers actively engage themselves, together, in the struggle against oppression of all kinds, in small neighborhood corners or all over the globe. Affiliation with a particular ecclesiastical group is a less potent determining factor for communion than is communion in the struggle for a just liberation. In eucharistic theology and practice today, the main trends toward ecumenical convergence come less from official circles concerned with sacramental control, and more from active Christians searching not so much for doctrinal accuracy as for individual and societal justice. One commentator on the Lima document puts a sharp challenge to what he sees as a definite lack in the present text. He broadens the notion of baptism and, in doing so, broadens the issue of ecumenism beyond strictly intra-Christian concerns.

> The text (of *BEM*) takes it for granted that the eucharistic meal is shared only among Christians, the baptized members of the churches (E 2, 27). Third world missions would raise the question whether the eucharist does not belong with all who are committed to and suffer for the cause of human liberation and justice which brought Jesus to the cross. Are not all who are thus committed far more deeply immersed (baptized) in the reality of Jesus than many who have received water baptism but have little or no commitment?[16]

Implicit here is a view of the core-reality of baptism. Baptism is not so much a ticket to ecclesial membership. It is *really* a conformity to the death-resurrection of Jesus Christ. As such, immersion into the Christ-event is immersion into commitment toward human liberation. Granted, the rules of logic do not necessarily allow the transposition that such commitment *equals* baptism. But, at least in some instances, they would allow for it as a logical possibility. Interesting observation.

4. Baptism, Eucharist and Ministry

If an ecumenical perspective pervades the Lima text, a broad liberationist perspective is no less operative. And both are rooted in the document's eschatological convictions. *BEM* clearly enunciates an ethical orientation. Baptism incorporates believers into a new life, to be effective in the midst of the present world. Christians

> ...acknowledge that baptism, as a baptism into Christ's death, has ethical implications, which not only call for personal sanctification, but also motivate Christians to strive for the realization of the will of God in all realms of life (Rom

---

[16] *Ibid,* p. 205.

6:9 ff.; Gal 3:27-28; I Peter 2:21-4:6). (*BEM,* Baptism III, Article 10).

The section on ministry insists that discipleship, which is the essence of ministry, calls for witness to the reign of God, a witness not unrelated to the human situation here and now. A public leader of the community never ceases to be one of its members. Together,

> The members of Christ's body are to struggle with the oppressed towards that freedom and dignity promised with the coming of the Kingdom. This mission needs to be carried out in varying political, social and cultural contexts...In so doing, they bring to the world a foretaste of the joy and glory of God's kingdom. (*BEM,* Ministry I, Article 4).

Even the office of *episcopos* appears in an eschatological light. "Every church needs this ministry of unity in some form in order to be the Church of God, the one body of Christ, a sign of the unity of all in the Kingdom." (*BEM,* Ministry III, Article 23).

Consonant with much current writing on the central Christian sacrament, the section on the Eucharist proceeds from a liberationist perspective. The Eucharist is a sign of what the world is to become: an act of solidarity, of sharing, of self-giving that knows no false boundaries. Fruitful participation in this central liturgical act demands one's engagement in the betterment of humankind. This is not simply because such engagement is a good and noble thing to do. Theologically, it is because the Eucharist uses created realities to be a sign of God's loving presence.

> The Eucharist opens up the vision of the divine rule which has been promised as the final renewal of creation, and is a foretaste of it. Signs of this renewal are present in the world wherever the grace of God is manifest and human beings work for justice, love and peace. (*BEM,* Eucharist II, Article 22).

It is because God so loved the *world* (not the church) that the Son came among us (John 3:16). Therefore, it is in our loving that same world that we meet the risen Lord, Son and sign of God.

When Christian sacraments are real and effective, then they are events which both bring to light and nourish the life-commitment of their participants, a commitment in service of personal and social liberation. When they are "dead," perhaps it is not because they lack liturgical planning and perfection, but because they truly *do* express a lack of concern for the evils of our world, they *are* a sign of commitment that is not there.

To recall the eschatological foundations of sacraments is to enter into the dynamic of the already but not yet, sign and countersign, confidence and struggle that marks lives lived in Christian hope. It is to enter actively into the task of building an earth more human, that it may be found worthy and ready, some day, for the all-transforming reign of God.

III. Supportive Readings

— Balasuriya, Tissa. *The Eucharist and Human Liberation.* Maryknoll, New York: Orbis Books, 1979.

> This Asian theologian examines the Eucharist out of a liberation perspective which rejects colonialism in any form. He sharply critiques all the feudal secular and ecclesial structures which have prevailed, even where Christianity has been the strongest. Balasuriya's condemnation of a "domesticating" socio-economic system is as devastating as any which emanate from the more well-known Latin American theologians today.

— Collins, Mary and Power, David, eds. *Can We Always Celebrate the Eucharist?* (Concilium, Volume 152). New York: The Seabury Press, 1982.

Written from an intra-Roman Catholic stance, these essays take a critical look at the relationship between Eucharistic celebrations and the life of the Christian community. They adopt many of the same directions of thought as we saw in discussing the factors affecting intercommunion. Questions of the distribution of power, reduction of the "explosiveness" of symbols, and prophetic vision take precedence over canonical regularity as norms for whether groups can or cannot celebrate the Eucharist authentically.

— Segundo, Juan Luis.   *The Sacraments Today.* Maryknoll, New York: Orbis Books, 1974.

This volume is part of the series, "A Theology of Artisans for a New Humanity." It proceeds from a Latin American liberationist perspective. Using traditional sacramental language, it poses challenging questions regarding the role of sacraments (oppressive or freeing) in Christian or, more accurately, human life.

— van Beeck, Franz J.   *Grounded in Love: Sacramental Theology in an Ecumenical Perspective.* Washington, D.C.: University Press of America, 1981.

Written in a popular style, this volume explores the commonalities shared by members of diverse Christian denominations. It is particularly interesting with regard to structural concerns, especially its interpretation of *validity.*

— Wainwright, Geoffrey.   *The Eucharist and Eschatology.* New York: Oxford University Press, 1981.

Wainwright uses his extensive knowledge of our biblical and theological tradition to explore the eschatological dimensions of one sacrament, the Eucharist. His method and basic insights might be applied to all. His is a very detailed, technical, scholarly study. Its value for ecumenical dialogue lies in the ecclesiological consequences which flow from the implications of his analysis.

7

Teaching Sacraments

In the course of this book, I have suggested ways of teaching sacramental theology which both students and I have found helpful over the years. The exercises, the readings, and the reflections have assisted me in working with seminarians, parish groups, clergy, and women religious. If any part of any chapter sparks a new thought, a fresh approach for others who teach and live our Christian sacraments, then the work will have fulfilled its purpose. In this final chapter, I want to explore further some of my own fundamental, though not always articulated, convictions. I shall attempt a synthesis of what I have learned from writing this book.

Teaching Sacraments is a title deliberately chosen. It has at least two different but related, two distinct but inseparable meanings. In a very real sense, we can speak of sacraments as teaching, as educating. In this regard, we may legitimately ask: what do they teach? and how? A second meaning surfaces, especially for those who consider teaching their vocation, their ministry. And that stems from the observation that, at its best, the educative process as a whole is sacramental. In the broad sense explored throughout this book, teaching is — or can be — a genuine sacrament. In what sense? how? These two foci provide the structure for this final, integrating chapter. For me, they express both the comfort and the challenge that *is* theological education today, in service of a more human, more Christian life tomorrow.

I. Sacraments That Teach

Ever since the Enlightenment and possibly before, western thought has been plagued by at least one false dichotomy which has special pertinence for us. Thought, learning and, therefore, teaching, emerged during that period as primarily if not exclusively rationalistic processes. Rigorous logic held sway. Technical and material productivity, the outcome of a strict "problem-solving" mentality, tended to diminish other values. Men, creatures of the head, held most professional teaching positions, certainly in institutions of higher learning, including seminaries. Women, creatures of the heart, were sometimes deemed worthy to teach young males, but only until they approached adolescence. Generally, women taught other females until they completed their education, whether in poor schools or in fashionable finishing schools. The structure was clear. Real learning was a matter of honing the intellect for sharp (even if sometimes sterile) argument and debate. Valued knowledge was the kind expressed in clear, univocal concepts. Applied with logical consistency, these would lead one to the truth of any matter.

While this broad picture runs the risk of over-generalization, it does pick up the educational mood of most western cultures, at least until recent times. Today, philosophers, educators, and scientists are taking a more wholistic view of the human person and, therefore, of human learning. Certainly, we are rational animals. But we are not exclusively so. And even our rationality is not an isolated segment, but rather an interpenetrating dimension of one complex whole. We learn both by discursive and by non-discursive experiences. We acquire knowledge, not simply by receiving information, but by *doing* things. David Tracy puts this shift toward a more inclusive approach in theological terms.

> A Christianity without a sense of radical participation in the whole...is a Christianity that has lost its roots in the human

experience of God's manifesting and revealing presence in all creation, in body, nature, in spirit, not only in history.[1]

In their use of the materials of the earth, the words of the human voice, and the gestures of the human body, sacraments are truly examples of the wholistic experience of which Tracy speaks and the wholistic teaching which educators strive for today.

A. THE IMAGINATION

Much of our current philosophical, theological, and educational speculation proceeds from a profound dissatisfaction with the Enlightenment model described above. Both psychological theorists and our own experience tell us that we do not live and learn on the level of clear ideas and precise logic alone. We live equally on the level of the imagination. At this point, I shall not attempt an exhaustive, ontological definition of this elusive but real human power. Rather, I propose the following operative description: imagination is the human mind's capacity to see meaning beyond what is immediately evident, to make connections among various individual components, and to envision possibilities. In a wholistic view of the person, reason and imagination are not rivals, not pitted against one another in a tug-of-war which neither side wins. Rather, they are mutually enhancing powers, mutually enriching dimensions of the one act of human existence.

Today, respect for the imaginative powers of persons is on the ascendancy. This stems from the observation that nothing new really happens, nothing is possible until we have first imagined it. It incorporates the recognition that mystery is a dimension of all human knowing, and that we approach the truth (and the truth approaches us) from many different directions. It admits the fact that image and sym-

---

[1]David Tracy, *The Analogical Imagination* (New York: Crossroad, 1981), p. 215.

bols shape our experience, vision, and values on levels deeper than that of mere explanation. They survive in us and affect our attitudes and actions long after we have "forgotten" them. Visions and images precede principles and theory, in the formation of human consciousness.

Clearly, this recovery of the power of the imagination is significant, both for sacramental theology and for educational methodology. By their very definition, sacraments are non-discursive symbolic actions. They speak to our senses and feelings as well as to our intellects. In Paul Ricoeur's familiar phrasing, they offer a "surplus of meaning," a field of understanding broader than a single dimension, wider than what immediately meets the eye. In their reverential use of material creation, they teach us that all life has meaning and worth derived from God's creative love, no matter the state of that life's "useful" productivity. Even in their imperfect, partial realization, sacraments teach that we are a union of spirit and flesh and, therefore, of glory and sin. Of course, all these realizations depend not only on faith, but on a "faithful" imagination. Insofar as symbolic knowledge is concerned, the imagination offers eyes that really see and ears that really hear what the symbols try to teach us.

The imagination is a powerful human faculty. Though stimulated by individual, particular sights, odors, sounds, and gestures, it always takes us beyond these particular instances and links us with more generalized, indeed a more universal human experience. Through a concrete image, a great poet can evoke in us a universal human experience of joy or sorrow, hope or despair. Through the strokes of a brush, the great artist can call forth from us our own moments of human failure or achievement, courage or fear. Central to any artistic process, the imagination always suggests more than it actually describes directly. Therefore, this human faculty is a witness to transcendence, to the "more" that lies beyond and grounds all human expression. It is a natural ally to the sacraments, those symbolic actions which call us to see in this loaf of bread and this cup of wine the ever-feeding presence of the Lord and to hear in the church's words of absolution the healing, reconciling words of our God.

1. Manifestation-disclosure

In *The Analogical Imagination,* David Tracy explores the polar tensions found in all forms of our Christian tradition, the pole of manifestation-disclosure and the pole of proclamation. Proclamation is the truth of prophetic critique, the judgment of "Yes, but. . ." handed down on anything human, lest it assume the place of God. Manifestation-disclosure is the truth of creation as an image of God, the sign of divine traces in our world. Its attitude is "Yes, and. . ." God does really come to and reveal God's self to us in and through human signs. Creation, rightly understood, does not deceive us. These poles correspond to David Power's categories of the "way of negativity" and the "way of affirmation," both of which must mark any religion which is neither idolatrous nor over-spiritualized. Though each pole must exist in all Christian denominations, the "catholic" strength has been in its emphasis on religion, including sacraments, as a manifestation. Human signs do disclose both God's revelation and human possibilities. Material creation does mediate God's infinite presence through finite forms. Revelation is always symbolic, always pointing to and incarnating the ultimate through the limited. Joined with our imaginative powers, the created order has disclosive power, the ability to tap into our deepest selves and touch the God already present there.

> In every human life there are certain privileged places, times, events, rituals, images, persons, which each of us recognizes as paradigmatic in their disclosure of some central truth by which we live. In Christian life the same kind of sense for the privileged, the paradigmatic also occurs.[2]

[2] *Ibid.,* p. 383.

For Christians, Jesus Christ is the decisive manifestation-disclosure both of our God and our humanity. The life of his church continues to reveal both who God is and who we are. Within that life, sacraments are paradigmatic moments of discovery.[3] In them, we learn the lessons that birth and death, desire and commitment, hurt and healing offer to us. Viewed and celebrated honestly, sacraments not only disclose the positive possibilities of existence. When they are authentic expressions of that existence, they also admit and reveal the alienation and oppression that mark individual lives and social systems marred by sin. At the same time as they demand our human striving and commitment, they depend on the prior reality, the disclosure of God's power as sheer gift.

2. Analogy

In order to learn the truth disclosed in sacraments, one must not only have imagination. One must have an analogical imagination. It is no accident that the great theologians of the catholic tradition, from Aquinas to Rahner, have relied greatly on arguments from analogy in their theological reflection. Analogy is the imaginative capacity to see and articulate similarity-in-difference, distinction with inseparability. It is that style of language and thought which illumines the meaning of one thing by its reference to another. Teachers rely greatly on analogy or comparison. They do so largely by searching for numerous concrete examples, especially when trying to communicate an abstract principle or idea. This is, first of all, because people come to learn or understand only by proceeding from *some* known to an unknown. By linking the unknown to the known, we come to know the former. By approaching the unfamiliar through the familiar, we and it become "at home" together. Secondly,

---

[3]The term *discovery* is deliberate. Consistent with the notion of God's grace as always, already present before we are ever consciously aware of it, we can say that sacraments do not "invent" God's presence in human life. They discover and bring it to light.

revelation (including God's) comes to people not first in abstract principles, but through concrete particulars. Newton's apple and the law of gravity; a 2 a.m. feeding and parental love; Jesus' parables and the kingdom of God: all are examples of the recognition of this fact. In learning, the concrete has a certain priority over the abstract. One particular focus is not merely an isolated, discrete instance meaningful only in and for itself. It is a genuine manifestation of the whole. In the language of James Joyce, it is an "epiphany." The secret of great artists, preachers, and educators is their ability to tap into the power of concrete images to illuminate human existence, wherever that existence is lived. They have an analogical imagination — the ability to stretch the limits of the obvious, to make connections sometimes ignored or forgotten, to "lead out" new meanings from old.

Whether or not we consciously advert to it, our church's sacramental life relies heavily on such an analogical imagination. Through this child's immersion in baptismal waters, we come to know God's gracious, unmerited (on our part) offer of grace for all. The sign of infant baptism teaches clearly that God loves all of us, adults included, before we ever come to express our own response of love. Through this anointing of a man surrounded by family, friends, and the medical staff who care for him, we learn the healing, blessing power of human touch. We glimpse the promised, supportive presence of God in and through these graced, flawed people of God. Through this couple's exchange of vows, we know that they are truly *present* in the very word they give to one another. Like God, in pledging their word they pledge their very selves. And for this moment at least, we know that commitment and fidelity are possible, even in our time.

B. PARTICIPATION

"We learn by doing." This maxim directly relates to the teaching power of sacraments. Sacraments are action-events. They yield their truth only to those who participate in them. This fact has two corollaries. First, sacraments demand active involvement, a theme explored above in our reflections on sacramental fruitfulness. A second corollary bears more detailed examination. Classical learning theories have held that knowledge influences action, that principles first learned intellectually are then applied practically. The model of religious and professional formation which kept people "out of the field" until they had sufficiently absorbed its theory illustrates this approach. And there is a certain validity to it, because the strong foundations upon which people built in the past have held firm for many, even to this day. But there is another side to learning theory. Behavioral sciences have challenged this classical approach, with an equal and opposite truth. What we do and how we act influence what we know. In his article exploring the positive challenges posed to our catholic richness today, Philip Murnion states the matter simply. ". . . people are as likely to act their way into a new way of thinking as they are to think their way into a new way of acting."[4] Murnion fears a new Gnosticism in the current valid but partial stress on conscious sacramental awareness and adult faith. Without wishing to fall into magic, he insists that the very action or power of sacramental celebrations themselves can move their participants, can create in them the dispositions necessary for fruitful encounter. Entering into and giving oneself over to their power teaches their truth. This is an important insight, and one congenial to the educative effects of symbolic events. What we do does shape our identities. The symbols to which we give ourselves over, religious or secular, do make our lives.

Participation is not merely a private, personal matter. It is not simply a question of individuals handing their isolated selves over to God's power working in and through signs. Sacraments are the church's signs. In our Christian tradition, participation is an act of *imagining with* one another —again, a manifestation of the self-transcendence which

---

[4]Philip Murnion, "A Sacramental Church in the Modern World." *Origins* 14 (June 21, 1984), p. 89.

community entails. Our sacramental system presupposes the power of a believing community to enable a *people* to become disposed to God's graceful action of which they are a part. This is why public, communal worship is not only useful but necessary. "...when imaginations come to life, people begin to make their own connections and juxtapositions. Together, we may arrive at strange new places."[5] In their sacraments, believers rehearse the great stories of their communal faith and enter into the action-events of communal transformation. Participation is their free response to a life, a story, a world, and a truth greater than any human expression. It is a precondition for any learning which the truth of God's symbolic presence offers.

C. THE POWER OF THE WORD

Words and verbal expression give access to reality. This is why totalitarian regimes burn books and silence thinkers. They know that, when people can express a thought, they can hold on to hope. They can spread that thought around. It can almost take on a life of its own, sparking the imaginations of others and — dangerous for the oppressive powers —inciting to courageous action. A great deal of teaching has to do with the power and limits of human words. Of all recent Roman Catholic theologians, Karl Rahner had probably given most attention to the significance of word and sacrament in relation to one another. While the motivation for much of his thinking has been the desire for a greater ecumenical rapprochement between Roman Catholics and Protestants, the results of his work are also useful for our educational interests. Rahner examines both the efficacious power of human words and the communicative power of human actions.

> ...since grace is the free personal self-communication of God, its divulgation is always free and personal and hence

---

[5]Kathleen Fischer, *The Inner Rainbow: The Imagination in Christian Life* (New York: Paulist, 1983), p. 154.

essentially word. Thus the whole sign of grace, no matter what form it takes, must partake of the character of the *word.*[6]

In whatever form God's grace exists in human history, that grace is both a communication and an action, both an effective word and a proclaiming sign. Its expression in the symbolic events we call sacraments is, in Augustine's phrasing, a "visible word."

Sacraments are words. They communicate, reveal, disclose something of God's hidden presence in human history. Therefore, they teach. They are effective words and therefore effective teachers, in that they bring about what they express. Through God's power, God's Word does what it says. In God, the medium *is* the message. God's Word *does* what God promises. Though any human action, including sacraments, falls short of the full expression of God's power, still the word-action link is real and must be maintained. Two Lutheran theologians join Rahner in their insistence on this essential identity.

> Theologically, there can be no gospel without sacraments, yet neither are the sacraments an addition to the proclamation. They are the acting-out side of the proclamation without which the proclamation itself does not occur.[7]

Sacraments communicate and the Word's proclamation effects. They are two dimensions of the same reality, the ever-effective revealing presence of God.

Sacraments not only teach us as mediators of God's presence in human history. These actions which use the things of the earth (water, oil, touch, promise...) teach us that creation is our common source and a world renewed our com-

[6]Karl Rahner, "The Word and the Eucharist." *Theological Investigations* 4 (New York: Crossroad-Seabury, 1974), p. 267.

[7]Carl E. Braaten, Robert W. Jensen, *The Futurist Option* (New York: Newman Press, 1970), p. 164.

mon goal. As actions not of individuals but of the church, they teach that ours is a common journey from that source to that goal. As a people we travel. As a people we are called.

D. LESSONS THAT NEED LEARNING

"Sacraments are for people." If we are true to this pastoral principle, then anyone interested in the educative role of sacraments has to ask a very practical question. What lessons does our world need to learn? If God's message is never arbitrary, indiscriminate information, then it is never unrelated to the world in which it is heard. We have already hinted at many of the needs of today's U.S. culture. In regard to the teaching function of sacraments, I would focus on two responses to those needs. First, it does not take a rock star to tell us that "ours is a material world." Unfortunately, the prevalent notion behind this materiality is one of acquisition, competition, and exploitation. A sacramental vision of life counters this narrowminded vision of material creation. It respects the inherent value and dignity of all life, precisely because God created it, Jesus entered into it, and sacraments use the things of this earth to express it. There is a permanent union between God and the world, expressed in the covenant-actions called sacraments. The "last word" in regard to this world is not exploitative pleasure or profitability. It is reverence. Our sacramental tradition teaches this lesson. God and the Christian community welcome babies, of no immediate productive value, into their midst as gift. They bless the sick, who drain both psychological and financial resources, for the truths about suffering that they can teach the rest of us. They present reconciliation not as weakness, but as affirming the possibility of converted hearts. They hold up marriage and orders as events that teach the goal of lives lived in mutual caring, not in mutual exploitation. Christians cannot afford to give our material world over to those who would profane it. That world is sacred. Our sacraments bear enduring witness to its holiness.

The second cultural observation is intimately linked with the first. Whichever comes first, the brand of selfish materialism described above goes hand in hand with an exaggerated individualism, a fragmenting tendency at the heart of modern society. Social scientists like Robert Bellah and Barbara Ehrenreich describe this situation of "me first, all others maybe." Christian ethicists like Margaret Farley explore the ethics of commitment. Pastoral theologians like Philip Murnion call for a new communitarianism, a measure of the *common* good that will contribute to making individual lives more whole, as well as making a more humane and just social order.

While all the forces of our critical intelligence need to be enlisted in the recovery of such a communitarian and interdependent vision, our Christian sacramental structure certainly has a prominent role to play. It is a ready-made resource. First of all, sacraments are the actions of a community called by God, a community formed not on the basis of human preference or convenience. This fact is instructive. Men and women, old and young, people of all racial, ethnic, and economic groups are invited into the Christian assembly. It takes all kinds. If sacramental communities are to be covenant communities, then they must be so as much with a recognition that God has called us, as with a recognition that we must enter into covenant with one another. While all sacramental celebrations are not necessarily moments of intimacy, they must necessarily be moments of solidarity, based on God's action in Christ on behalf of all people. "We are tempted to find the Lord in the affections of the intimate when the Lord says he will more likely be in the desperations of the stranger."[8] In this community, inclusiveness is less a matter of feeling good about one another than it is a question of overcoming and reconciling our differences. This is a lifelong task, one that makes the death-resurrection of our baptismal rhetoric real. Our sustenance during this struggle is the Eucharist. Among other things, the theology of the Eucharist is a theology of sacrifice. Sacrifice affirms the

[8]Murnion, *op. cit.*, p. 88.

holiness of Jesus Christ's self-giving unto death on behalf of all people. The Eucharist will become real for us, only as we affirm and enter into the sacredness of self-giving on behalf of others ourselves.

II. Teaching That Is Sacrament

For any teacher, the temptation is to explore the educational enterprise from her or his personal and professional perspective. Though my own biases and insights obviously inform the following remarks, I have tried to concentrate more on what the process of learning reveals and, most important, on the primary agent in any educational dialogue, the student. Hopefully, through this indirect approach, what the teacher can be in this process shall emerge. But teacher and teaching stand always at the service of the greater reality, the person who "goes beyond" where he or she is, and thus truly becomes one who learns. Like it or not, all teaching is a sign — a sign that forms, reforms or, in some cases, deforms those who receive it. For me, the following pages serve as an examination of conscience, a set of criteria against which to ask the question, "Of what is my teaching a sign?"

A. TOWARD A THEOLOGY OF EDUCATION

Theorists have written volumes on philosophies of education. To my knowledge, few if any have explored education from a theological perspective. Our topic of sacraments provides a good entry point for such an endeavor. Because, when it works, education exhibits many of the characteristics of these sign-actions.

1. Revelation and Grace

In contrast to its corresponding document from the first Vatican council, the document on Revelation from Vatican II insists that God's revelation is not primarily propositional, not truth about something arbitrary, outside the believer's own experience. Nor is education. While there are facts to be learned and principles to be assented to, education is not "news from nowhere," not a message extrinsic to the human person. Whatever the discipline, it is about ourselves and the world, physical and social, in which we live.

Rahner comments on what God says (teaches) to people in revelation.

> God does not say all sorts of things to men, and his words are not a miscellany of disconnected subjects. In the last resort he utters only one thing, which is himself as eternal salvation in the Spirit of the incarnate Logos of God.[9]

God communicates *saving* truth to people, a message which makes a difference in their lives because it is about the depths of their lives. So too does education, especially theological education. When it works, this event is not simply *didache* but *kerygma,* not merely instruction but proclamation. God's Word (*dabar*), the reality being studied discloses itself. Like revelation and like the sacraments, effective education becomes an "exhibitive word," rendering present and visible in the lives of those who learn something of what is taught.

In revelation, God's grace always precedes its external, historical expression. Grace is the condition for the possibility of a faith-response, the reality of God's presence always, already in the human heart, before the head ever knows and names it. People, events, and symbols tap into that grace and bring the dimly-known awareness into the light of self-knowledge. Analogously, education too taps into what is already there — abilities, experiences, prior learning, even lacks. The effective teacher has an imagination sufficiently rich to *educare,* to lead out and articulate what is already known. In that articulation, new meanings emerge. This is probably why most of the effective educators I know, from

---

[9]Rahner, *op. cit.,* p. 278.

preschool through graduate level, use a number of examples to illustrate their point. Examples take the common-place, the ordinary, the generally known and link them with what is apparently unknown but waiting to emerge into consciousness. "Oh yes, I see!" Like a good preacher, a good teacher develops an existential imagination, the ability to draw from the many resources in her or his own knowledge in order to touch and awaken the knowledge in others. The existentially imaginative teacher learns to see things with others' eyes, to walk in others' shoes, in order to help others to name, and therefore claim, their own understanding.

2. Creation: God's Revelation in the Ordinary

The use of examples referred to above leads us into our next consideration. Normally, when teachers and students give examples, they pick illustrations from ordinary life. Ordinary life is where people live out God's gift of creation. The catholic sacramental system especially affirms this truth. Its seven signs correspond to those typical moments which mark people's lives: birth and death, commitment, healing from hurt, support, and sustenance. By and large, most people lead rather undramatic lives. They meet God, if at all, in the everyday grace of their everyday existence. They know God's creative love, if at all, in their own efforts to put order into chaos, to let there be light, and to live as God's image day by day.

Education too is an arena of the ordinary. Occasionally, some persons engaged in it make brilliant discoveries and formulate world-shaking insights. But by and large, the process of teaching and learning is very prosaic, as prosaic as life itself — and just as important. This enterprise exhibits all the possibilities that our created existence offers, and all its limitations. Its daily discipline of class sessions, schedules, and assignments is, for those who learn to view it as such, an ascetical exercise and an experience of our created finitude. As creatures, we are "thrown" into a world of situated freedom. We have neither infinite time nor unlimited space. There is a beginning and an end to every human project, including exams and papers and our favorite class. The secret of life is to come to terms with its necessary limits, all the while seeking to expand its unnecessary ones. In T.S. Eliot's words, we creatures pray that our creator will "Teach us to care and not to care." We hope to learn what to cling to in life and what to let go. Entered into openly, education gives ample opportunities for learning the difficult and glorious lessons of our creaturehood.

3. A Community of Learners

In its revised rites, Vatican II highlighted the essential factor of community in any sacramental celebration. Recently, theologians have begun to explore seriously the theological significance of the liturgical assembly. By its very existence, an assembly of believers witnesses to the fact that just as no one celebrates alone, so no one goes to God alone. An assembly of learners offers the same witness. Whether in a classroom, a community room or a parish hall, people gathered together become co-learners with as well as co-teachers for one another. Education is not only a two-way street, where professional teacher and individual learner mutually enrich one another. It is a many-pathed route, where all those involved are, simultaneously, contributing to and receiving from the knowledge of all the others. As with the liturgy itself, this emphasis on mutual influence has been among the weakest, both in educational theory and practice. How often, when one student questions or speaks, others "take a breather," knowing that for this brief moment they don't have to take notes because they won't be tested on the material. And yet, if God has called us as a people (and all the plural addressees in the Scriptures attest to this), then we have to take one another seriously. When the educational environment is a good one, when people are relaxed and mutually respectful, then they really do reciprocally enrich one another. Their varied experiences teach varied insights, articulated in a variety of ways. One of the most effective exercises in a group is free association, or the expression of what different people think of when they hear a given word, see a given image, etc. It contributes to the development of a communal imagination, richer and broader than that possessed by any individual on her or his own.

4. Symbolic Activity

The theological rationale for a community of learners is not its ready provision of a cozy, affirming group. Rather, this rationale is rooted in the nature of individuals as partial possessors of the truth. We need one another to learn the whole of life, because no single one of us has a corner on its meaning. As it is with people, so it is with people's symbols. While these signs are powerful, they also exhibit the partial character of all things human. Viewed positively, this means that they are multivalent. Viewed negatively, it means that we humans need all the signs we can get, in order to discover the truth of ourselves and of our God.

Education is an eminently multivalent, multifaceted process. In any ordinary classroom experience, the teacher does not have the luxury of an author who, in writing, can develop and argue for a single overriding theme. Consistency of logic is not always the highest value here. Granted, one hopes not to foster inconsistency. But education is more like a spiral than a straight line. The teaching situation must be eclectic. While they do proceed from a given set of assumptions toward a given goal, teachers must bring in whatever helps this process. That generally includes many different examples, as we noted above. And, if teaching is not to be ideological, it incorporates many different approaches. While some educational theorists can be purists in regard to educational methodology, I don't know too many practitioners who can afford to be so.

Viewed theologically, education is a moment in the mystery of human life, as distinct from the "solvable problem" of that life. Every and all moments are partial, not simply because they are pale, weak, and ineffective, but because life — and learning — are endlessly intelligible. Our sacramental instincts know that. We repeat certain ritual moments, because no single celebration can ever say it all. In theological education, we repeat the great human themes of God and humankind, joy and suffering, good and evil, death and resurrection — again, because no single expression of these truths can say it all.

Like all symbols, including the sacraments, education not only expresses who we are. It makes us who we are. If we are what we eat, we are no less what we learn. This shaping power of education is the force behind such movements as Head Start, Jesse Jackson's PUSH, and the tenacity of religious schools that stay in economically disadvantaged areas. It is the motivation of those who persevere in the profession, with all its problems, over the long haul.

Another aspect of education's symbolic power concerns the teacher very directly. Somewhere along the line, I caught the truism: What you *are* speaks so loudly to me that I cannot hear what you are saying. In all disciplines, especially those most explicitly dealing with human and religious values, teaching is a risky business. The risk is the radical danger of one's self-exposure to others. Like sacraments, teachers and their teaching need to be authentic. This does not mean that anyone ever perfectly matches her or his message, especially when that message is the gospel of Jesus Christ. But there must be a relative coherence, a congruity between the medium and the message, the teacher and the taught. This is a very humbling thought. Anyone who stands up within a group and presumes to teach the great mysteries of her or his tradition is on display. The teacher of theology is as much in the spotlight as those ordained to public leadership. If and when we utter what we have not pondered in our own hearts, not struggled with, and do not believe — it shows. What is inside does indeed come to external expression. Insofar as we are able, educators must be vigilant that the inner word of our own grace and the external expression of our proclamation come together and be recognizable as one. We must, first and always, be hearers of God's Word, before we ever dare to try to teach it.

B. THE EDUCATIVE PROCESS

Much of what we might say about the educative process is implicit in the remarks above. But two issues deserve further exploration. We approached them earlier, in considering the sacraments as manifestation-disclosure and as covenant-dialogue. We return briefly to them here, for their instructive value regarding the process of education itself.

1. Manifestation-disclosure

Like sacramental activity, education is a process of recognition, an experience of "coming home" and seeing the familiar in a new way. It is a gradual unfolding, an opening up, a bringing to clearer light of what is already there in human life. Analogy, examples, and anecdotes contribute greatly to this process. So does poetry. Many times, the concrete images of a poem powerfully illustrate the sometimes abstract content of a theological concept. The universal can and does speak through the particular. I usually conclude any course or series on sacraments in general with a poem. One that is especially effective is the title poem from John Shea's collection, *The God Who Fell From Heaven.*

A Prayer To The God Who Fell From Heaven

If you had stayed
tightfisted in the sky
and watched us thrash
with all the patience of a pipe smoker,
I would pray
like a golden bullet
aimed at your heart.
But the story says
you cried
and so heavy was the tear
you fell with it to earth
where like a baritone in a bar

it is never time to go home.
So you move among us
twisting every straight line
into Picasso,
stealing kisses from pinched lips,
holding our hand in the dark.
So now when I pray
I sit and turn my mind
like a television knob
till you are there
with your large, open hands
spreading my life before me
like a Sunday tablecloth
and pulling up a chair yourself
for by now
the secret is out.
You are home.

From *The God Who Fell From Heaven* by John Shea. ©1979 Argus Communications, a division of DLM, Inc., Allen, TX 75002.

Whenever I read these lines aloud to a group, its members respond with nods of recognition. All the Christological affirmations of God's enduring presence come to rest here. All the mystery dimensions of human existence, the surprises, the "always, already" of grace and graciousness, the lavishness of nurturing love find simple but eloquent expression. The Incarnation's message of God's active, non-detached participation in ordinary human lives leaps off the page.

2. Covenant-dialogue

Sacraments express the mutual covenant, the dialogue, the rich relationship between God and people. If they are to be valid, if they are to yield their meaning and power, then they require active participation, at least in the sense of being willing to give oneself over to their possibilities. So too with education. Both teachers and learners *are* both teachers and learners. In the exchange of information, insights, and ignorance, a covenant is forged. If students have a hard time admitting they don't know the answer, how much more difficult it is for professional educators to do so. And yet, what lessons are taught and learned when we do. What mutual trust is fostered.

While liberating education encourages as critical, objective, and open a stance as possible, most educators today admit that total objectivity and neutrality is an impossible illusion. There *is* a passion appropriate to the educative process. We learn by participation, by actively (giving ourselves) over and entering into realities, movements, and truths larger than ourselves. Bored, blasé sideliners can pass tests and get credentials. They may even get ordained. But they do not really learn, especially in a discipline that is about commitment—God's and ours. The excitement of learning increases in proportion to our wholehearted involvement in the process. Theology yields its truths to those who not only grasp those truths, but allow themselves to be grasped by them.

C. THE GOAL OF EDUCATION

1. Communication as Transformation

"Words, words, words." "Not everyone who says to me, 'Lord, Lord,' shall enter the kingdom of heaven" (Mt. 7:21).

> The truth of Christ exists only as concrete realization, which means: the verification principle of every theological statement is the praxis that it enables for the future. Theological statements contain as much truth as they deliver practically in transforming reality.[10]

Education is "about" a lot of words. Yet, these words are never for their own sakes. Communication has a goal. That goal is always some kind of transformation. As it is with God's self-revelation and with the Church's symbolic actions, so it is with teaching and with learning.

---

[10]Dorothée Soelle, *Political Theology* (Philadelphia: Fortress Press, 1974) p. 76.

2. *Sign and Countersign*

This goal of transformation is expressed by the categories of *sign* and *countersign*. Sacraments both affirmatively express the goodness of the human condition and call that condition forward, to be transformed into its real vocation, a "new creation." Education has the same eschatological structure. Theological instruction is not simply to communicate facts and to convince logically. Its goal is to awaken faith to action. We are and are not the same when we have learned something new. Students tell me that I frequently use the phrase, "Yes, but . . ." It is an acknowledgement of affirmation and negation at the same time. Yes, baptism is about birth. But it is also about dying. Yes, the Eucharist is about food and feasting. But (how instructive for our world) it is also about fasting and famine. Marriage is about the beauty and creative power of sexuality. But it is also about the ordinary ups and downs of family life, the rights and responsibilities of all family members. Anointing is about hope and healing. But it is also about a pastoral care of the sick which must confront disease, health-care delivery systems, and the allocation of healing resources throughout the world. Education is about admitting both what we know and do not know. In the words of two books by the same twentieth century author, teaching is both a conserving and a subversive activity.[11] It is a sign of the good things that our culture has to offer, and a prophetic countersign to the tendency to settle in and settle for one insight, one ideology. If education is *liberal* in any sense of the word, it must free individuals and communities from any idolatry, even a "worthy" idolatry like religion. In its pursuit of truth, it must stop at no single expression of the truth, no matter how attractive, no matter how satisfying.

D. THE RESULT: A LIFELONG LEARNER

The ultimate measure for whether or not teaching is sacramental is what happens in students. In June 1985, I parti-

---

[11]Neil Postman, *Teaching as a Subversive Activity* (New York: Delacorte Press, 1969) and *Teaching as a Conserving Activity* (New York: Delacorte Press, 1979).

cipated in a panel discussion of "Theological Education as a Theological Problem" at the annual meeting of the Catholic Theological Society of America. I shall rely heavily on that presentation for my concluding reflections. In preparation for the panel, I posed the following question to a number of students: What has your theological education done for you?[12] From their varied responses, I learned that, when it works, theological education is an experience of self-transcendence: that basic human dynamic of being drawn beyond ourselves toward a reality, a truth, a horizon greater than we are, the mystery in which we live, move, and have our being.

The varied dimensions of this self-transcendence emerged in three major themes. The first is a disposition, a basic openness to change and be changed. One student spoke very concretely, describing his experience of theological education as a "shaking loose. At my arrival, I threw everything up in the air. When they came down, I picked up the pieces. And they fit together in a totally new way." Another spoke of "an unfinished process that shapes and unshapes us, if we allow its power to penetrate our lives." Such attitudes reveal a lack of rigidity, an openness to risk, to the otherness of the reality we encounter when we move outside ourselves, allowing ourselves to be transformed. Theological education works with men and women open to receive its questions as their own.

The second common theme in this self-transcending process is the element of dialogue or interaction. First, students described the importance of dialogue between and among the community of learners engaged in this enterprise. One called faculty "people who put nuggets in my head." Some might balk at this, seeing it as a negative example of the "banking" model of active teacher and passive learner. Faculty might rather be persons who help students to discover the nuggets that are there. Still, the man meant his image in a positive sense. "Nuggets" are riches to be mined, and not without strenuous effort. They are valuable. They may not all pay off during the years of formal theological

[12]See Patricia Smith, R.S.M. "Theological Education as a Theological Problem IV." *CTSA Proceedings* 40, 1985, pp. 78-82.

study. But, under the pressure of life and ministry, they will be discovered, when their cash value is needed.

My inquiry affirmed the importance of dialogue and interaction among students themselves. They placed great value on processing together what they were learning. This exchange became a concrete moment in which to recognize, reconcile, and appreciate the differences among one another. The participants had to go outside themselves, to risk having their knowledge and attitudes challenged and corrected. How necessary this is, if all people, including the church, are to function well. Students' personal struggles to appropriate truths ever ancient, ever new mirror the church's struggle to preach its universal message to people of particular places and times. This communal effort is a healthy model, especially for men and women seeking to internalize what being God's people and what collaborative ministry is all about. It is also a welcome countersign to the excessive individualism which is the original sin of our time.

The third common element marking theological education as an occasion for self-transcendence focuses on the material of study: the presuppositions which determine one's initial approach, the facts confronting those presuppositions, and the direction of thought and action to which one's study may lead. In this regard, I recall my own first Scripture course. Cherished certainties were exploded. Long-held absolutes went the way of long-held absolutes. And I had to discover new anchors, more able to stand firm amid the pounding waves of historical criticism. As a teacher, I found the students' observations on this dimension of theological study most exciting. They had a real appreciation for the faith-purifying possibilities of the historical-critical approach to Scripture, sacraments, theological and magisterial statements. They saw the life-giving connection between solid knowledge and healthy devotion. In a paper written for a class on Mary, one student described what had happened to him in the course of his study. His words speak more eloquently than mine.

> I began with the wrong approach. . .narrow. . .relating every-
> thing to a single, important, and valid theme. . .I had pre-
> decided what was going to be useful and what no longer
> applied for me today. . .At some point in the process of this
> course, with hardly a moment of recognition, my approach
> changed. Rather than relate the information to my already-
> formed category, I simply let the knowledge speak on its own
> behalf. . .in its own context.

This testimony illustrates the truth that the way we interpret determines what we allow to happen. Letting the facts,
the tradition speak on its own behalf drew this student out of
his preconceived, personal, relevant framework. He let the
challenge of Biblical exegesis, historical relativity, and theological images change him. He allowed the context, the how
and why of particular historical emphases, to speak to him.
He had begun his study of Mary with one emphasis, a very
valid and contemporary one at that, Mary as disciple. But he
transcended this one image to the richness that variety
offers, to an appreciation for the complex human process
that is tradition. He picked up on the major theme of the
role of imagination in theology by confessing "that theology
is an art as well as a science. The beauty of images being
evoked which go deeper than words or pictures could possibly explain is something which I had lost in my need to
define and categorize. The life had become stifled by the
process, rather than letting the process enliven."

At some mysterious moment, by some mysterious connection, this student went beyond his own familiar world, into
new territory. One of his peers describes that going beyond
by the image of "innocence" — not naive inexperience, not
polyannic optimism, but the enduring moment of "always
moving into unknown territory." That is not a bad image for
the fact that, no matter how many new lands we enter, we
enter them as innocent, as always new.

These students' insights remind me of the words of Joseph
Sittler: "Learning disorganizes and complicates the stifling

simplicity of the purely personal."[13] To learn is an act of faith, in that we give ourselves over to consequences that we do not know. Like the philosopher Pascal, we wager that God will be there at the end.

In a paper written for a Biblical course, another student described well the process of theological education as a dialogue between our self-consciously recognized prejudices and a particular text. He described the act of interpretation as testing out and critiquing our guesses, seeing the text function as "a tool that allows us...to dialogue with the sky," a dialogue from which meaning emerges. The sky is that which is beyond our reach, but always beckoning. Rahner might call this image "the Whither of transcendence." In this case, the object of interpretation is a Lukan parable. The student comments: "The meanings the parable could have had are in conflict with the meanings we want it to have. Out of this conflict, the ineffable voice of God can be heard speaking afresh to the listener." He cautions against absolutizing any single method of interpretation. If we take seriously the paradoxical nature of revelation, then "there is an undeniable riddle quality (to parables) that cannot be explained away by allegory *or* by form criticism." Parables are "paradoxical, mysterious, inviting, confusing. If they are to be in any way revelatory of the Mystery of God, they have to be. Such is the nature of a God who is both immanent and transcendent." Education is the process of honing our ability to recognize and live with that riddle.

The insights expressed above witness to openness to the "other" of the reality we meet in and through the study of theology. They attest to the experience not only of grasping truth, but of being grasped by it. In theological truth, if anywhere, there is always more. Two thousand years after the fact of Jesus, we continue to research and write because no one formulation, no single image can say it all. In David Tracy's words, the best we have is "a rough coherence, a

---

[13]Joseph Sittler, *The Care of the Earth and Other University Sermons* (Philadelphia: Fortress Press, 1964), p. 143.

relative adequacy." Each new and partial insight becomes a new starting-point, a fresh stimulus to examine the truth and beauty ever ancient, ever new, revealed and hidden at one and the same time.

The process of giving ourselves over to a reality greater than we are corresponds to the traditional category of grace — a grace which, in Rahnerian terms, is always and already present before we ever reflect upon or name it. As noted in an earlier context, good education is like good preaching. It taps into and puts words of recognition on human experience. When you are teaching and a connection clicks, you can see it in students' eyes. Like a sacrament, the educative process brings to light what lives in the dim shadows. One student put the result of his learning this way:

> Perhaps I knew this before the course. Or perhaps I had experienced it but never took the time to reflect upon it in detail and put it into words. In either case, the end result is a vigor, a renewed appreciation for the connection between theology and devotion, head and heart.

Without knowledge, we are captive to the comfort of the familiar. With the thirst for knowledge, we can risk setting out together on the self-transcending journey of pilgrims. We can become who we are: men and women who do not really rest until we are at home in the deep and broad mystery of God. Teaching which facilitates this journey is truly a sacrament, an effective sign of God's faithful, challenging presence. Teachers who, even once in a lifetime, learn this lesson, are fortunate indeed. They receive a disclosure of the meaning of their vocation, their call to serve the truth which makes people both free and freeing, both enabled and enabling. And, like the God who invites them to share in this co-creating work, they see that "It is very good."

Index of Proper Names

Index of Subjects

Analogy, 29, 43, 68, 123-124, 170-171, 183

Anointing and Pastoral Care of the Sick, 29, 36-37, 50, 54, 76, 95-96, 98, 102, 115-116, 137, 144, 171-175, 186

Baptism, 20-23, 27, 36-37, 48-51, 59, 70-71, 83, 89, 96, 98, 102, 107, 116, 118-119, 121, 123, 125, 130, 132, 143, 149, 158, 161, 171, 186

Baptism, Eucharist and Ministry (Lima Document, Faith and Order Paper 111), 139, 142, 145, 147, 149-150, 158, 161-162

Bible, 31-32, 63-66, 72-77, 111-112, 126

Book of Exodus, 65-66, 94

Book of Genesis, 62, 72-77, 93

Book of Isaiah, 105-106

Causality, 27, 110, 118-119, 123-125, 129-130, 134, 138, 148, 150

Church, 21-23, 34, 41, 71-73, 82, 84, 89, 96, 104, 107, 110-138, 148, 151-152, 156-164, 170, 172, 175, 188

Classical (Scholastic) theology, 11-12, 26, 32, 38-39, 67, 79, 99, 108, 110, 120, 124, 138, 139

Clergy, 25, 28

Confirmation, 76, 118-119, 123, 130, 143

Constantinian era, 24

Constitution on the Liturgy (Sacrosanctum Concilium), 32, 131

Council of Chalcedon, 90, 92

Council of Florence, 121

Council of Trent, 121, 126-127, 129, 132

Counter-Reformation, 124-126, 131, 134

Covenant, 62, 64, 73, 77, 79, 93-95, 125, 133, 143-144, 155, 175-176, 183-185

Creation, 21, 62-64, 68, 74-77, 93, 101, 103, 113, 145, 150, 162, 167-169, 174-175, 179-180, 186, 191

Death-resurrection, 21, 92, 96-104, 140-141, 159

Declaration on the Relationship of the Church to Non-Christian Religions (Nostra Aetate), 81-82

Decree of Gratian, 120

Decree on the Church's Missionary Activity (Ad Gentes Divinitus), 77

Decree on Ecumenism (Unitatis Redintegratio), 77

Dogmatic Constitution on the Church (Lumen Gentium), 31, 77, 81, 112

Eastern Christianity (Fathers), 26, 67

Ecumenical issues, 121, 126, 131, 141-154, 173

Efficacious (effective) signs, 27, 46-47, 59, 73, 75, 82, 126, 134, 137, 139, 163, 174, 178, 191

Election, 113, 129

Enlightenment, 14, 166-167

Eschatology, 139-164, 186

Eucharist (Lord's Supper), 20-23, 27, 29, 35-37, 48-49, 51, 53, 55-57, 59-60, 76, 83, 89, 95-96, 98-100, 102, 116-117, 120-121, 123, 125-126, 131-132, 135, 143, 150, 152-154, 157, 159-160, 164, 168, 176-177, 186

ex opere operantis, 110, 133

ex opere operato, 110, 118, 124, 133

Faith, 99, 105, 123-124, 128, 132-134, 151, 186

First Letter to the Corinthians, 88, 100-102